The Little Book of Ethics

A human values approach

Whether we find it uncomfortable to talk about ethics or not, it is a central part of our lives. It is as basic and pervasive as thinking and feeling. And it is not just what keeps us compliant with the law, it is the gateway to the quality of our relationships and the spiritual fulfilment of our lives.

The Little Book of Ethics introduces us to ethics through the lens of values, and offers us five core human values – honesty, peace, right action, love and insight. It shows how these values are applied in different domains of our lives, and relates them to six aims of human life, where ethics is united with meaning and purpose.

People do not all see ethics from the same perspective, and the book describes seven levels of consciousness, ranging from the shamelessly selfish survivalist through to the exemplar of global harmony. This framework enables us to see why people talk about ethics differently, and also shows us how we can develop our understanding and strengthen our virtue.

Discussion of ethics can fall into a variety of traps. It can be simplistic, pious, doctrinaire, bombastic or quaintly philosophical. *The Little Book of Ethics* is simple in conception but sweeping in scope. It is offered as a practical handbook for establishing the grounds on which you can live a worthwhile life.

The Little Book of Ethics

A human values approach

Glenn Martin

G.P. Martin Publishing

The Little Book of Ethics

By Glenn Martin

Published 2011 by G.P. Martin Publishing

Websites: www.glennmartin.com.au

                www.ethics.andvalues.com.au

Contact: glenn@glennmartin.com.au

**National Library of Australia
Cataloguing-in-Publication Data**

Author:	Martin, Glenn.
Title:	The little book of ethics : a human values approach / Glenn Martin.
ISBN:	978 0 9804045 4 8 (pbk.)
Subjects:	Ethics. Values.
Dewey Number:	170

Book layout, design and photo by the author

Typeset in Garamond 12 pt

Printed by Lulu.com

Look from the place
where we are all one,
carry the light into the day,
stay open in the heart.

There are two things in life: joy and correctness.

Contents

Preface

In writing this little book, my question was: can I say something simple but helpful about ethics? There are many books on ethics, offering a great variety of perspectives. My intent here is to offer a framework for thinking about ethics that can be used by both ordinary people and leaders, in their lives and at work. It does not require the reader to subscribe to a particular set of beliefs about God or the nature of the world. Mine is an experiential approach to life and human behaviour.

My envisaged audience is as wide as you can imagine. My aim is for the concepts in this book to have resonance for people everywhere, across all cultures, religions and societies. I believe the human values approach described here provides the foundation for a worthwhile life for individual persons, groups, organisations and societies.

I hope that any insight you gain from this approach will inspire and sustain you to live ethically. It is often said that the world is crying out for people and leaders whose lives are deeply rooted in moral principles, values and ethics, and who have regard for the well-being of others rather than grasping selfishly for their own gain.

Of course this has always been true; it is ancient wisdom. And it is possible for each of us today to be such a person or leader, whatever our situation. Indeed, being ethical, as you will see in this book, leads us on to the fulfilment of all that it is possible for us to be. The ethical life extends far beyond mere obedience to rules.

The Little Book of Ethics follows my book *Human Values and Ethics in the Workplace*, which was a more academic account of the concepts presented here. The latter book gives more depth on how this framework of concepts emerged.

Chapter 1:
How to start talking about ethics

> Although all stable societies rest firmly on a consensus of values, invariably the individuals in those societies prefer not to discuss those values, except in glittering generalities, not because they are unimportant, but because they are so important that to discuss them seriously might open them to question and reinterpretation.
>
> L.E. Modesitt Jr, *The Ethos Effect*

In some ways it is easy to talk about ethics, because everybody agrees that we should be ethical. We could even go a step further, and say that we agree on certain ethical values. We should be honest, for example, and we shouldn't hurt others.

We can go another step, and say we should keep to these values, even in circumstances where it might be hard to do so. The consequences for ourselves might look undesirable – we might lose our job, or a promotion, or miss out on some money. Or the pressure to do what we think is unethical may be strong – friends and colleagues expect us to do the act, they might demand it of us. But we think of an ethical person as one who is able to resist such pressures. That seems to be an essential element of ethics in practice.

Then people come up with words and arguments to explain why certain actions, which it might be suggested are unethical, are acceptable. For example, the action might seem dishonest, but the argument goes that this is how business is done. If we didn't perform these actions, our business would fall apart, competitors would ruin us and we would go broke. And everyone knows this is how things are; they expect it, they accommodate it, they adjust.

So very quickly, the simple question of ethics gets complicated. What do we talk about now? We can still talk about ethics, but is it just empty words, hypocrisy? And when we hear people talk about ethics, and high human values like honesty and service to the

1

community, are they so clean? We know that some people build their fortunes on blood and dishonesty, and once they are rich, they want to preach love and kindness to everyone.

If this is how things are, perhaps it is simply foolish to be too concerned about the ethics of our own actions. Others are doing what they can to serve their own interests, even lying to us about their commitment to honesty and fairness while they are busy achieving their business ends by lying and cheating. Wouldn't we be fools to stick to the rules?

We can persuade ourselves that there is weight in all these arguments. But if this is how we decide to act, we have to ask one final question: what does this make of us? That is to say, what do we become when we give up on ethical values? Do we like ourselves? Because we haven't really given up on the values, or rather, they haven't given up on us. We still know when we are hurting someone. It's just that we have placed a big justification between us and our acknowledgment that we are doing an unethical thing.

Our conversations about ethics become clearer if we distinguish between three different orientations towards ethics:

1. My personal ethical standards: Can I live with myself? Am I living in accordance with the highest values I know?

2. My relationships with people: my group, organisation, family, the stranger: Do my actions contribute to positive relationships with other people?

3. The laws of the society I live in: What behaviour is required or prohibited by the law?

Many conversations about ethics become confused because people don't distinguish between these different orientations, or see that they can result in different behaviour in given circumstances. We will not be able to explain behaviour, or establish guidance for our own behaviour, unless we distinguish between these different orientations. They give us different reference points for our own actions, and what we might have to say about other people's actions.

Motivations for ethics

At the root of behaviour lie beliefs about the nature of ourselves and the world, and consequently, attitudes towards how we will live in the world. These beliefs and attitudes become embodied in our values, which by nature are quite stable over time – not set in stone, but it takes a significant event or shift in perspective to change them.

We also need to consider the influence of vision. Our values are not just a reflection of how we see the existing world, they are also a reflection of how we would like the world to be. What is the ideal society? In the *I Ching*, in hexagram 48: The Well, the ideal society is described as a society of great harmony in which the leader and the people work in full cooperation and with unity of purpose. People of ability are chosen for positions of responsibility, there is mutual respect among people, there is justice, and there is an understanding of what nature provides and the need to live in harmony with its cycles.

This vision can be expanded at length, and cover any aspect of life we choose to consider. To the vision of an ideal society we can add a vision of the ideal way of life for an individual person. And we can individualise the vision to our own interests and perspectives. The point is that we all have a vision of how we would like life to be, even if we have not articulated it. It is implicit in our thoughts, words and actions.

When we take this whole bundle – our perceptions of the world, our beliefs, our attitudes, our values and our vision, and add to that our needs – we end up with motivations that affect how we act in relation to ethics. And likewise, so do other people. And of course, individuals, and groups, organisations and societies, are different in all these respects. We act according to how we see the world, and so do other people.

Is ethics relative?

This perspective raises questions about whether it is possible to have any meaningful conversation about ethics. I think this; you think that. It's all relative. Who has the right to say what is right?

Breaking the conversation down into the three different orientations as we have done above gives us a way of having a conversation. If we only have the first orientation – my personal ethical standards – then if we disagree there is no way to resolve things. But if we realise that groups (and societies) come to certain agreements about ethics, then we can have a conversation about what we think are appropriate standards for our group.

Once we have embarked on that conversation, we see that groups and societies also establish sets of rules, policies or laws, that formalise agreements about ethics. An example at society level is consumer protection laws, which seek to protect individual consumers against unscrupulous tactics that businesses might use to cheat them out of money.

It is a dynamic situation; laws are likewise seldom set in stone. The conversation always continues, as situations change, new experiences occur, new conditions arise and perceptions evolve. Rules, laws and policies are refined, modified, reversed, replaced, augmented. We don't say that this means that ethics is relative. We say, rather, that the group, organisation or society is engaging in a continuing effort to formulate rules that align with and promote its vision of the ideal.

There is an overarching perspective to these conversations, that is to do with whether we are pessimistic or optimistic. Our perspective could be determined by the belief that people are essentially selfish and the world is an ugly jungle, and people in power make the laws only to serve themselves. My task in this book is to offer a framework that suggests that our optimism is justified.

We can, in fact, say even at this point that seeking to live ethically is worthwhile. Why? Because even if it were true that the world was a vile place, you still have to live with yourself. And you might experience life better if you live ethically, because it grants you some dignity, even if that turns out to be only in your own eyes. However, what we will say offers a much more inspiring vision. Nevertheless, it is good to know that in the darkest of scenarios, you could maintain your integrity even there.

The starting point: responsibility

There is a starting point for ethics, and it is that you accept the notion of responsibility for yourself. What does "being responsible" mean? Politicians often make a show of "accepting responsibility" but it doesn't seem to have any consequences. They carry on as usual.

Responsibility means that you accept responsibility for your thoughts, words, and actions, and you are accountable for your thoughts and words and actions. You do not say, when you come to consider some wrongdoing, failing or shortcoming, that you couldn't help it, or everyone does it, or you had no choice, or it wasn't really that bad. You do not seek to evade your accountability for your actions with excuses and denials.

Being responsible has a backward-looking aspect and a forward-looking aspect. Looking back, it means having remorse for wrongdoing we have done or harm we have caused. It also means accepting punishment and making whatever recompense we can for the harm caused. Looking forward, it means we undertake not to act in the same way again.

You might recognise the influences and pressures on you, from your peer group, organisational norms, or from your upbringing or your natural inclinations. You may recognise the fears that drive you or the great desires you may have. But to talk about ethics you have to acknowledge that you bear responsibility for your thoughts, words and actions, and that you exercise choice.

This point is fundamental, and it is worth spending a day or a week simply observing yourself in relation to the acceptance of responsibility. If you scrutinise yourself with utmost honesty, you may be disconcerted by how hard it is to be fully accountable for your words and actions throughout the course of an ordinary day. We are all extremely well-trained at diverting responsibility to others and not acting in accordance with our words. Blaming others is an easy and constant temptation, but it puts up a block to and precludes any meaningful discussion of ethics.

Chapter 2:
Ethics as a restraint on behaviour

Moral principle restrains one's behaviour.

I Ching, Hexagram 60: Jie, Restricting (Alfred Huang's version)

Suppose, then, that we accept the notion that we are responsible and accountable for our actions. We might still feel resentment about ethics. It might seem that ethics is a restraint on us, something that continually holds us back from our full freedom. The quote above from the *I Ching* says that in a sense, this is an accurate description of ethics. So wouldn't we be better off without it?

It helps to have an analogy. Think of a motor bike. There are two important things about riding a motor bike. It has to have power, and it has to have steering. If we just rev the engine and don't steer it, we will smash into any obstacle that comes up. Steering is what makes riding a motor bike useful, and fun. Power alone is aimless and invariably destructive, of both the self and others.

A crude analogy, yes, but still apt. Applied to persons, we can see that we have power. Just being alive means having drives and desires. We don't have to invent them or artificially generate them; they are just there. We naturally want to do things, achieve things and obtain things. And we can take the attitude that we will allow nothing to stand between us and getting what we want. We can probably think of people who attempt to live this way – single-minded, goal-focused, but brutal and expedient.

So ethics operates as the steering. It modifies our actions and steers them in particular directions so that we are not ineffectual or destructive in our actions to attain goals. This is the first point – we do need to restrain, or guide, our behaviour in order to attain goals.

This idea of two aspects that complement each other to create a viable whole is represented in the yin-yang symbol. Yin and yang are

6

not opposites – they do not oppose each other – but both are necessary to create the viable whole, the circle that represents eternity, or sustainability. Here, power is yang (male energy, initiating) and steering, the modifier, is yin (female energy, nurturing). The idea that power needs a complementary aspect was recognised by Martin Luther King: "Power without love is reckless and abusive, and love without power is sentimental and anaemic."

So we need something to modify our power. Power needs a bridle, just as a horse needs one if we are to ride it. But is it ethics? Is the bridle more than the fact that our actions need to be strategic instead of random and blind?

There are deeper arguments. One argument is that the agreements of society about ethics provide strong reasons for us to restrain our behaviour. Society determines that certain acts and behaviour damage the society if they are allowed to pass unpunished, so it creates laws. That makes it prudent for us to restrain our behaviour. Now we have two types of restraints: (1) modify our actions to ensure they are strategic, and (2) modify our actions to ensure that we do not break the law and attract punishment.

We can add another type of restraint as well. When societies decide that certain acts should be prohibited and offenders should be punished, it generally means that people disapprove of those acts. To take a simple example, stealing is illegal and people generally disapprove of a person who steals. So as well as the legal risks involved in stealing, there is the risk of attracting the disapproval of other people if we steal. This is a third type of restraint on our behaviour.

But not breaking the law is not a moral principle, it might simply be acting prudently. And not doing illegal acts because we do not wish to attract people's disapproval is not a moral principle either. It is still a matter of being prudent. To go back to the quote, it is moral principles that are said to restrain our behaviour. And we are making the assertion that ethics is essential.

The argument that ethics is essential is different to the arguments above. When we say that being strategic is prudent, we could test it out by doing some research. We could have a sample population and a control group, and apply different conditions to each and record the outcomes. We could analyse the data and draw conclusions that could be generalised to the whole population. The closing statement could be something like "a high correlation was found between acting strategically and attaining goals".

Could we do this for "acting in accordance with moral principles"? Many researchers have tried, and some have delivered conclusions they say are significant. For example, the financial performance of companies has been tracked on the basis of their commitment to ethics codes and ethics training. In many cases the results have been promising – it seems that there may be a positive correlation between the explicit actions of companies in relation to ethics and their financial success in the markets.

And yet.....if that conclusion was invariably true, haven't we just reduced ethics to an act of prudence? What if the opposite had been found? Would we want to advise companies that it was **not** in their interests to act ethically?

The essence of moral principles is that they are not modified in accordance with worldly outcomes. A famous example is from the 1980s when Johnson & Johnson's product Tylenol, a pain reliever, was implicated in the deaths of several people over a short period. The product had been tampered with, and cyanide added, but it was not known who did it or how.

Faced with the evidence, did it respond by saying it valued human life, but $100 million was too high a price to pay to pull the product off the shelves? Johnson & Johnson took the position that its products were intended to enhance life, not put people at risk of being killed, and it withdrew all of the Tylenol from the market until the problem was solved. That is what a moral principle is. It is not something that is up for sale or negotiation. It is not conditional on favourable financial outcomes.

The end of the Johnson & Johnson story is that the company's reputation as a trusted provider of pharmaceuticals soared, and when Tylenol came back onto the market, it easily recaptured its market share, and the company's subsequent profits far surpassed their former level.

But to emphasise the long-term financial success of Johnson & Johnson's actions is to miss the point of the story. When the company pulled the product off the market, it sustained an immediate, huge loss, and there was no promise of recovery. If you were one of the executives making this decision, you could not have argued that you knew things would be alright in the long run. You could not have argued that your proposed course of action was prudent or strategic. You were simply facing an immediate loss. All you have at that moment is your moral principles restraining your behaviour.

Yes, you can still argue the point. You could say that killing customers was not in Johnson & Johnson's best interests in the long term, so they were in fact acting prudently. Their reputation was the foundation of their future success. But then you could find other companies who had a different attitude towards moral principles, and were less troubled by deaths among their customers or workers (for example, manufacturers of tobacco and asbestos products), and you would have to examine whether or not their fortunes were affected by their attitude.

Would you reach a compelling conclusion, either way? Our view here is that ethics is not a question that is subject to empirical proof of positive financial outcomes. That is not what it is about. Rather, beyond all the empirical and circumstantial evidence that acting ethically may serve your worldly interests, ethics is an act of faith, an assertion that this is how you choose to live as a human being, as a person, or collectively, as an organisation or society.

When we say that moral principles restrain our behaviour, we are saying that we are making the choice to restrain our own behaviour on the basis of ethics. All the other arguments for acting ethically are still present and carry their weight – we refrain from illegal acts because we might get caught and punished. Or we behave ethically because we want the approval of other people, or because it will build a relationship that is in our interest. But beyond this, acting ethically means to act in a certain way simply because we see that it is the right thing to do and it is how we want to live.

However, can we say that ethics is essential? Couldn't we just as easily choose to live without ethics at a personal level? Couldn't we be satisfied just to obey the law and do enough to retain the approval of other people? Beyond that we will act purely to serve our own interests….?

Chapter 3:
Why ethics is essential

All life is a struggle with ethics. Those who fail to understand that are doomed to destruction.

L.E. Modesitt Jr, *The Ethos Effect*

In the context of business and the workplace, it seems like a bold step to say that ethics is essential. There are many who still maintain adamantly that the only responsibility of business is to maximise its profits. In terms of workplace relationships there are many who would say that ethics is ultimately a subjective matter – it is individual and personal – so in a collective context we have to be satisfied with externalised rules and policies.

The "solely for profit" argument is naïve at best. But it is better characterised as an ambit claim. The person who says business has no responsibility beyond profits is conveniently forgetting a host of conditions on which it relies to exist. The most important of these is trust, a condition that arises out of the mutual commitment of stakeholders to ethical behaviour.

In recent years, around the world, we have seen that when political regimes have fallen or been overthrown, it is extremely difficult to do business in those places. When there is no solid foundation of the rule of law, and by extension, there is no shared commitment among the business community to fair, honest (ethical) business, the marketplace becomes dominated by rogues and thugs. And eventually, when the society stabilises, the rogues and thugs are reined in, driven out or punished.

So, in stable societies where there are laws regulating business conduct, and the laws are at least notionally enforced, even when business people talk tough about competition they are relying on that bedrock of moral restraint which is manifest in the legal framework. Of course, in their unbridled enthusiasm for competitiveness (or rather, winning), business people are going to say things like "Business only exists to make a profit". That is to be expected.

We should simply recognise that such statements are not arguments in any sense; rather, they are ambit claims. An ambit claim is when someone makes a claim that they know is nonsense ("I should have all the lollies") and they don't expect you to believe it, but wouldn't it be fabulous for them if you did?

What we are saying, then, is that the functioning of groups and societies depends on a certain level of shared commitment to ethics. We might get a grudging acceptance of this proposition from some of those who advocate that business should be free of restraint. What they might say now is that the restraints should be minimised so as not to discourage healthy competition.

In other words, they seek to quarantine the scope of ethics. The same intent is at work when people say that ethics is subjective; they say that in collective contexts we have to restrict discussion to external rules that we can agree on. To a point, this may be fine. But it should be acknowledged that we do not get to any agreements about what the rules will be without first having a discussion that is about ethics. Ethics is an inherent part of human activities and relationships.

There could be an objection to this point: the critic could say that we are only talking about ethics (to give an example, say false advertising) insofar as it is needed for the marketplace to work properly. We are not interested in ethics as such. But to follow this point, when we determine that a company has engaged in false advertising, it has to be accepted that we are asking an ethical question: has it lied to customers? Ethics is in the room; it is a question of how we justify pushing it into a corner and restricting its application.

Suppose we try to address the business person's insistence that the intrusion of ethics into business should be minimised. The argument is that business success requires drive, innovation and agility, and somehow, ethical rules get in the way. The business person wants the freedom not to have to think about all those rules.

This is an issue that relates back to the three orientations towards ethics that we mentioned earlier. One orientation saw ethics as being only about the law, and this fits our business enthusiast. He/she is not interested in the other two ethical orientations – a concern about relationships with other people, or a personal commitment to high ethical standards. Again, this sounds like an ambit claim. "Ethics interferes with my need to be agile" sounds very much like "I should have all the lollies".

The heart of it: valuing as an integral aspect of the functioning of our minds

So far we have said that ethics seems to be essential to human activity, in the sense that social functioning depends on a certain level of shared commitment to ethics. We cannot, for example, have a marketplace that works if unethical acts such as cheating and thuggery are allowed to go unchecked.

There is another side to the proposition that ethics is essential, and this gets to the heart of what we are as humans. This is, that evaluating things is an ever-present, ongoing activity of the human mind. Our mind is constantly perceiving and evaluating things, from the physical aspects of our surroundings through to judgements about our own and others' behaviour.

Is it too hot or too cold? Do we like this or not? Are we attracted or repelled? Is it good or bad? Is it true or not true? Is it desirable or undesirable? This function, of valuing, is a constant stream in our mind, from which arise our ideas about what is ethical and unethical. We become quite sophisticated about this activity, and we can make very fine distinctions – we develop a spectrum of valuations rather than remaining at the level of crude yes/no judgements.

When we say that ethics is essential, we mean that this function of valuing is an integral aspect of our minds. We do it anyway. To say it is not applicable in a particular sphere of life, as some people in the business world try to do, is to deny what our mind constantly tells us. As long as people perform actions that affect other people, and the earth, our minds will evaluate them.

We evaluate from many perspectives. The scope of the valuing function covers all the aspects we are interested in, in relation to any given topic. We might be interested in the financial success of a company, its efficiency, its innovation, or the effect of an action on the market for particular kinds of goods. Any aspect we like to think of is subject to exploration by the valuing function of our mind.

Are some of these aspects off-limits in the business world? That is, can businesses ignore some of the judgements that might be put up about certain aspects of their behaviour? As was indicated above, when businesses make such a claim, it should be regarded as an ambit claim. It should be subject to open scrutiny and debate.

What makes matters ethical?

Our concern at the moment is, what is it that makes a matter ethical? What is it that distinguishes ethics from aspects that we would agree have little or no ethical intensity – say, matters of style, preference and taste?

When we talk about ethics it is common to use the words 'good' and 'bad', and 'right' and 'wrong', and these are useful words **within** a discussion about ethics, once we have established what we mean by ethics. But we have to set our criteria first. Outside of a context, the terms 'good' and 'bad', and 'right' and 'wrong' are not helpful to clarity.

Our view is that ethics is based on the idea of well-being. To act ethically is to act out of concern for the well-being of others. Ethics is our sense of obligation to consider the well-being of others as well as our own well-being. It extends to consideration of the well-being of society and the natural world which sustains us.

So, what makes matters 'ethical' is that they are matters concerning how the actions of a person affect the well-being of another person or the natural world. Saying this does not take away the complexity of ethics in practice, but it does provide a clear, solid starting point for discussion of ethical matters.

Chapter 4:
Ethics as regard for the well-being of the world

The universe is everlasting.
The reason the universe is everlasting is that
it does not live for self. Therefore it can long endure.
Therefore the sage puts himself last,
and finds himself in the foremost place,
regards his body as accidental,
and his body is thereby preserved.
Is it not because he does not live for self, that his self is realised?

Lao Tzu, *Tao Te Ching*, verse 7 (trans. Lin Yutang)

The starting point for ethics is that I see myself as a person who exists in the world, along with other people. I exist in the context of my body, my close social relationships (family, friends, colleagues etc), the broader social context of society, and the broader physical context of the natural world. As a person, I can take responsibility for my thoughts, words and actions.

In this context, ethics arises as my sense of obligation to have regard for the well-being of other people and the natural world. Then we come to see that our actions serve the well-being of others when we act in accordance with certain values. And given that we exist in a social context (I exist among others), we come to see that the well-being of people is best served when we all abide by these values.

Accordingly, we move quickly beyond particular instances. Instead of continually asking the question, will this action serve the well-being of others?, we hold that their well-being is served when we act in accordance with a set of values. For example, benevolence is a value that is held in high regard in many cultures. Alternatively we could refer to love, magnanimity, sympathy or compassion.

So we say that acting ethically means to act out of regard for the well-being of others, and we do this when we live in accordance with a set of values such as benevolence. Different cultures give prominence to different values, although what is more remarkable is the amount of similarity there is between the value sets of different cultures. Benevolence is recognised, for example, as the supreme virtue by Confucius, love is the exalted virtue of Christianity, and compassion lies at the centre of Buddhism.

In the next chapter we will explore values and present a model of the person that shows how there are five core human values, from which all other values arise. Our interest in the present chapter is to understand the essence of the commitment to live ethically.

We can approach this by asking the question, what if we chose not to live ethically? What would this mean? At its heart, it would mean that we were choosing to live without regard for others; we would have regard only for our own interests. We would live selfishly. As we said earlier, "moral principle restrains one's behaviour". A life lived without the restraint of ethics is one that is lived to serve the ego.

The practical consequence of the ego-centred life is that we perpetually cater to the desires and fears that the ego presents to us, and the desires that are pushed upon us in our commercialised, consumption-focused society. We seek to accumulate more and more money, possessions, artifacts and status. We struggle to take for ourselves far more than what we need, in a world of scarcity. We look after our own interests even when it means acting unfairly, dishonestly or corruptly, even when it means creating suffering for others.

We might say we are not that as bad as all that, that we do moderate our actions, or that we are not as bad as some people. Be that as it may, each time we allow the ego and selfishness to determine our actions rather than regard for the well-being of others and the natural world, apart from the immediate effects of our actions, we contribute to the pattern, the culture, of unethical behaviour in our society. So how do we understand ego, and how do we live with it?

Living with the ego

Ego is an endowment of nature, it is an indispensable nucleus for the formation of a finite personality. The ego looks towards separateness and independence. Yet, within the finite personality there is an impulse towards oneness with all-that-is. The ego helps us to differentiate ourselves as individuals as we grow up, but then it is as if it becomes headstrong and wants to take over altogether.

The lesson we need to learn about the ego is how to continue to develop as an individual without letting the ego run out of control. The ego is always externally oriented, it wants to possess, to dominate, to consume. The paradox is that to bring the self to realisation, we need to transcend the ego. The self only comes to realisation when it serves the well-being of all. The ego values external things, but the true self values being in integrity, living honestly, being faithful, fostering justice, caring for other people and being at peace with all-that-is. The paradox is that it is only in this way that we may become all that it is possible for us to be.

It may seem that this is an idealistic picture of the self, one not realisable in ordinary life. But living ethically is the endeavour to become what is our real nature, our true self, not the pursuit of some far-off dream. To live ethically is to gradually grow into the self, and to become attuned to all-that-is. Unselfishness is the central moral virtue, from which all others proceed.

We cultivate unselfishness when we recognise the emotions that the ego plays with. With awareness we can see when we are drawn towards greed, indulgence, self-importance, vanity, arrogance, we are drawn into anger, fear and anxiety, and we find ourselves acting cruelly and uncaringly. Being ethical involves reinforcing the emotions of positive regard for the well-being of all, and disciplining and containing the divisive emotions that drive us blindly towards selfish ends. In so doing, over time we strengthen our character, our virtues.

Is this agenda far more than our society demands? Perhaps, and yet the business world is coming to recognise that if a business is to be sustainable it must look beyond short-term advantage and ask what kind of behaviour establishes the ground for long-term viability. And what does this mean for behaviour if not acting in a way that builds trust? So even if the quest for the self seems too lofty, the case for behaving ethically is still strong. The people who plan business strategies, devise policies and build organisational cultures need to consider what kinds of emotions they will foster – those of selfishness and fear, or those that enable cooperation and trust.

The rhetoric of change is one factor that undermines ethical conduct. The business environment is depicted as one where the environment is constantly changing and the factors in success are continually shifting. In this context it is easy to think that ethics is likewise variable and relative, and the only rule is "whatever works".

We do not have to view the world this way. The ancient wisdom is that the world as a whole is unchangeable, but in its manifestations it appears to constantly change. If we understand this then we may indeed be powerful; to understand it we need to grasp the whole, and see that it is our focus on the fragments, the parts, the ephemeral, that has beguiled and bewildered us.

The challenge for leaders is to discover, to get the feel for, the unchangeable whole within the flurry of trends and moving parts. Ethical work or ethical management is actually the pathway to seeing the whole and how it works. A constant focus on serving the well-being of the whole enables us to see how to act in myriad different circumstances.

Acting ethically, moreover, committing oneself to being ethical, takes trust in the fact that we ourselves will be sustained. We cannot do that until we disengage ourselves from worldly ambition. The true self is not dependent on external things like wealth, social status, popularity or power. The commitment to ethics means that we commit to doing the right thing anyway. We trust that we will be taken care of.

This is not a sacrificial approach to life; it is not a martyr's creed. Just as we look at other people and expect them to do what they can to look after themselves, so we too must do what we need to do to look after ourselves and our loved ones. The key is that we do it without the attachment that the ego has to external rewards or to the fear of ruin. The measure that the true self always uses is whether we have acted with regard to the well-being of others and to the whole.

Having regard to the well-being of others is an attitude of giving. It is in contrast to the grasping that is the way of the ego. We are so conditioned to the practice of striving for money and clinging to it, and using it to consume for ourselves, that we forget that whatever we get is a gift of the universe and the well-being of others is fostered by the gifts that we give to them. Unethical behaviour is restrained when we see that the world works by the exchanging of gifts – we prosper because we are the receiver of gifts and others prosper because we are the giver of gifts.

The attitude of giving and being grateful for what we receive generates a feeling of oneness with all, whereas the selfish grasping of the ego leaves us feeling separate and isolated. That sense of isolation breeds fear, jealousy, envy and anxiety, and is the source of much unethical behaviour. We need to educate ourselves into sympathy, into the feeling of oneness with other people – their true selves, not their fearful or belligerent egos.

There may be differences between cultures, but as humans we share common needs. The unchangeable common ground between cultures is these common needs. The ethical human is the one who transcends ego concerns and strives to realise and express their humanity, their true self, by serving the well-being of all.

Many cultures in history have had the vision of the leader who is a person of wisdom who serves the well-being of society rather than their own personal appetites. In this vision, the world of commerce plays a subservient role, existing to fulfil the physical needs of society and thereby enabling it to pursue the higher interests of harmony, learning and joy.

It is customary to believe that we have severed ourselves from that past, and that commerce is the vivifying energy of our society. If this is so, it seems strange that so many employees are disenchanted with their work and unhappy with their leaders. And while corporations are generally eager to attest their commitment to ethics, it is not so easy to see how they seek to put ethics into practice in business or the workplace. When called to account, corporations typically retreat to the defence that what they did was legal.

Chapter 5:
Five dimensions of the person and five core human values

It is the awareness of self that makes it possible to have values.

Pierro Ferrucci, *What We May Be*

The beginning of ethics is the acceptance that we are responsible for our actions. As a person, as a human being, I am responsible for my thoughts, words and actions and the effect they have on other people and the natural world. What is entailed by responsibility will be explored further in Chapter 8.

The essence of ethics is to act out of concern for the well-being of other people and the natural world, and to restrain the demands of our ego which would disregard their well-being.

Having established this as the foundation for living ethically, we can take a closer look at the nature of persons. In doing so we will build a framework for what it means to live ethically. Our nature as persons leads to a set of five core human values, from which all other values are derived. Given that these values are connected to the nature of what we are as humans, these values make sense across different cultures, religions and societies.

To introduce core human values, we can first of all acknowledge some general aspects of our experience as persons. Figure 1 is a depiction of a person, represented by an iceberg. It shows the exterior and interior views of the person. It draws attention to the fact that there are aspects of ourselves that are visible to others, aspects that are not observable by others but are available to our consciousness, and aspects that are below the level of our consciousness.

Figure 1: A model of the person – exterior and interior views

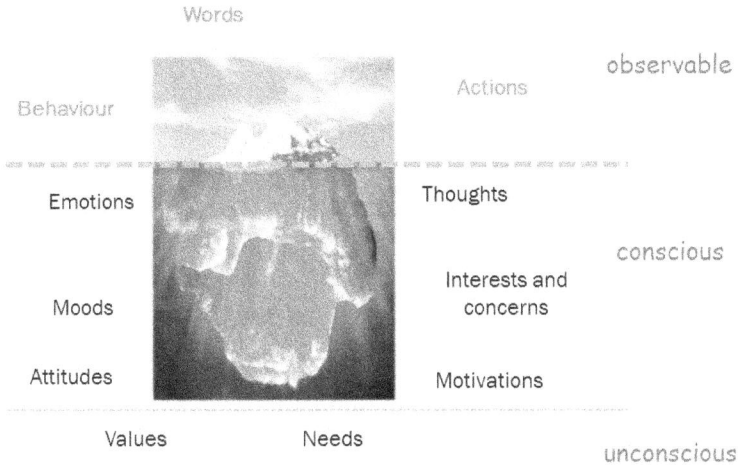

To talk about living ethically and being responsible, we need to have this image in mind. There are many implications that can be drawn from the image. One implication is that when we are thinking about whether another person's words or actions are ethical, we need to bear in mind that there is a great deal that we cannot observe. We can only surmise what internal factors (thoughts, moods, motivations etc) preceded the person's action.

A comment that needs to be made about the figure is that it is not intended to be interpreted rigidly. The division between what is conscious and unconscious, for example, is not rigid, and it may be different between one person or another, or different for one person at different times. Values are shown as unconscious, because many people are only dimly aware of their values. Yet values can be brought into consciousness.

The figure simply seeks to point out that there are aspects of our mind that are not immediately open to us. It may take reflection, self-observation and feedback from others before we can identify our values, or even our mood or attitudes.

There is also a great deal of overlap between the concepts presented – emotions, moods, interests, motivations, etc. That should not

21

concern us too much. Most of the time we manage to use the words appropriately; we know they are connected and yet distinguishable concepts. But given that our endeavour here is to identify core human values, we have to be aware that values sit among the other concepts in our minds.

Values are distinguishable most simply as the things that are important to a person, but the meaning is stronger than that. To hold something as a value is to consider it worthy of esteem for its own sake. Values are conceptions of what is desirable. Accordingly, they influence what people choose to do, and how people evaluate actions.

The difficulty with identifying a set of values about which we might all be in agreement is that there seem to be so many values, and it might seem that almost anything can be called a value. Our interest in this book is in values that relate to ethics. So we can narrow the field somewhat. For example, values that relate to matters of style, preference and taste are not our primary concern here. Nor are values that relate to basic physiological and social needs such as personal safety, health, sense of belonging, tradition and pleasure.

When we say these values are not our primary concern, we do not mean that we are ignoring them. Not at all. Rather, we are saying that we can assume that these things are all present, they are part of what humans are; we do not have to invent them or argue for them. So when we come to ethics, we know that the point of ethics is that it may modify actions that we might want to take in furtherance of one of those values, be it pleasure, sense of belonging or whatever.

We can also set aside values related to competence and power, which would include things like ambition, achievement, leadership and expertise. These are also part of the human condition. Ethically, in themselves they are neutral.

Having narrowed the field down, we want to identify values that have ethical import, and we want to know whether there is any internal sense to the values we identify, or is it just a mystery that certain values are about ethics? We can approach this task by thinking about common models that we use to depict humans. One of these models is the one that sees persons as consisting of body, mind and spirit. This is not something we try and prove. It is not "true"; it is simply that sometimes it can be a useful way of conceptualising the different aspects of a person.

Another common model consists of intellect, emotions and will. Again, this can be a useful set of distinctions, as long as we do not become committed to them as separate and competing entities. Recent research into the brain and the mind cautions us that these aspects are integrally connected to each other and are involved with each other. Our intellectual activity engages our emotions, and our emotions recruit our intellect. Nor does our will act alone; it is a compatriot of the emotions and the intellect.

A model bears some useful relevance to reality. Its value is that it can take something that is vast and complicated, and represent it simply, and yet still accurately. It resonates with our experience of the actual thing. It helps us to understand key features of the reality.

Five-dimensional model of the person

With this in mind, a model is presented here of the person. It holds that there are five dimensions of the person. These five dimensions are a useful way of understanding our experience, our grounds for making decisions, our actions, the projects we undertake, and our feelings.

It is not the only model that can be devised to represent our experience. Other models might focus more on spiritual development, or psychological aspects of the person. A psychologist might be more interested in levels of consciousness, and how dreams and the subconscious feed into our conscious experience. A spiritual enquirer might talk of higher consciousness and the collective unconscious.

Our focus is on the role of values in human behaviour, and the five-dimensional model is aimed at illuminating that role. Students of psychology or spirituality may be interested to explore how this model sits alongside of their models.

The five dimensions are named as follows:

- Cognition
- Emotions
- Moral Valuing
- Spirit (also called Energy)
- Psyche (also called Identity)

How do we explain these dimensions? You see that one dimension, moral valuing, focuses explicitly on ethics, but this dimension does not exist in isolation. It exists within the context of the other four dimensions. They support moral valuing, they enable it, and they give it sense, because we are both material beings, creatures located in a physical world, and at the same time, beings who have thoughts and feelings that move us to speak in the language of the spirit and the psyche.

The story of the five dimensions of the person can be told in this way.

Dimension 1: Cognition

We are creatures of the physical world, and we develop the use of our faculties (sight, hearing etc) so as to operate effectively in this worldly context. We develop knowledge, memory and logical reasoning so that we can be competent in dealing with the material world. This is the dimension of Cognition.

Dimension 2: Emotions

Although our cognitive skills are essential to dealing effectively with the physical world, we realise that we are also creatures of emotion, and unless we are aware of our emotions and can manage them, we will not be effective. If we are but "slaves to our passions" then we will do harm to ourselves and others. We need to harness our fierce emotions – our anger, lust, fear, desire – and learn how to express our tender emotions – caring, cheerfulness, peacefulness – in order to be able to interact with other people constructively and build relationships. This is the dimension of Emotion.

Dimension 3: Moral Valuing

In recognising emotions, we come to see that some situations we encounter raise particularly strong emotions, and they relate not only to our own welfare, but to that of others. Thus we come to develop the notions of fairness, justice, dignity and respect. These qualities are specifically ethical, because they relate to our concern for the well-being of others. This is the dimension of Moral Valuing.

The three dimensions described so far provide an adequate account for many purposes. We can talk about the aspects that come into play when we are trying to deal with the practicalities of living in the material world – where we exercise our cognitive dimension. And we can recognise the influences on our behaviour that come from the fact that we are creatures of emotion, and we moderate these two dimensions with ethical values such as fairness and respect.

But when we look into emotions more deeply, we may see that there are emotions of a distinct type. In the Emotions dimension our primary concerns are with managing our emotions so that we can manage ourselves and interact constructively with other people. If we look more deeply, we see that some of our emotions could be described as being related to spirit. Rather than being concerned primarily with productive relationships in social contexts, they are about deep connections between people as spirit.

Dimension 4: Spirit (or Energy)

The word "spirit" is used here in the sense of "the vital principle or animating force of a living being". When people begin to operate consciously on the basis of the first three dimensions, an energy begins to develop that is evident in individual experience and in interaction with other people. When people have got to the stage of working and relating together competently, harmoniously and ethically, a spirit develops where they can appreciate that something is being created that has energy, that has a life and is of value. This is the dimension of Spirit.

Dimension 5: Psyche (or Identity)

There is one further dimension, in fact, the one that makes sense of all the others. When people have activated the four dimensions above, then something further is possible. It is possible for a sense of identity and purpose to develop. People begin to see that when cognition, emotion, moral valuing and spirit are functioning well, they have evolved a sense of their own uniqueness. Moreover, they can exercise awareness of what is being created and consciously shape its nature. They can now speak of identity. This is the dimension of the Psyche.

Representing the five dimensions

It is useful to depict this constellation of dimensions visually. It helps to see how they are built up and how they relate to each other. Figure 2 represents the five dimensions of the person. Each line represents one of the dimensions. The first three dimensions – Cognition, Emotion and Moral Valuing – are shown as a triangle, and the fourth and fifth dimensions – Spirit and Identity – are shown as two lines layered over the top of the triangle. This is intended to convey what has just been discussed, that Spirit and Identity augment the first three dimensions and extend their meaning.

Figure 2: The five dimensions of the person

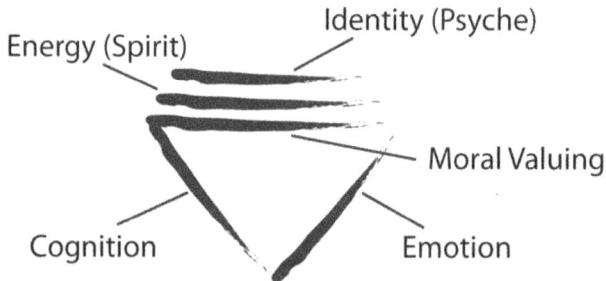

The first three dimensions are shown as an inverted triangle for a reason. The concept of left brain-right brain functioning has become well-known. The left brain is the rational, logical kind of functioning, while the right brain is about emotional, intuitive functioning. It makes sense to assign the left line to Cognition and the right line to Emotion.

Then Moral Valuing serves as the line that completes the triangle. The figure is intended to emphasise, more strongly than words can, that cognition and emotion are incomplete without the intervening role of moral valuing. In any situation or decision-making context, these three elements are engaged. To fail to recognise any one of them is to operate in a less than optimal way.

Energy and Identity are shown overlaying the top of the triangle because this is how they fit into our functioning. The first three dimensions are basic. It is when they are all recognised and they are all functioning well that we see the emergence of energy, or spirit (these terms are interchangeable in many instances).

The two dimensions of Energy and Identity bring life to its fullness. They also illustrate that ethics is not the province of petty people who are absorbed in pedantic rule-keeping. Ethics is the province of those who seek to come to terms with the full breadth and complexity of what life may bring our way, and who seek to know and live out the highest human values.

One observation we can make about this account of the five dimensions of the person is that it suggests there are a number of values at stake in any ethical decision, not just one. It is not just a matter of a single value, say honesty, fairness, or caring. All of the dimensions are present, so the values that may come into play concern the values relating to all of the dimensions.

Although we have started from the bottom and worked our way upwards, it is also possible to start at the top and work down. If we start with the idea of awareness of identity and purpose, we are open to seeing the spirit dimension of experience, the flow of energy that occurs when we seek to live out our purpose in the material world. And if we continue on this journey, we will see that we have to make decisions about ethical issues, we will have to learn how to manage our emotions, and we will have to deal constructively (that is, rationally and intelligently) with the material world.

The core value of each dimension

We can associate a core value with each of the dimensions. If the five dimensions give us a useful, and universal, account of the person as human being, then what we have is a framework for five core human values, that can be understood across cultures, religions and societies. The framework may take different nuances in each context, but it constitutes a set of concepts that speaks to what we have in common: that we are all human beings.

These are the core values associated with each dimension:

1. Cognition: Truth
2. Emotion: Peace
3. Moral Valuing: Right action
4. Spirit: Love
5. Identity: Insight

We will explain why each of these values is the salient value for its dimension. We will then expand the explanation to give a whole constellation of values for each dimension. The core values are intended to be the flag-bearer for the dimensions, not to exclude the other values or act as a synonym for them. The whole set of values is needed in order to get a comprehensive picture of what is meant in each dimension. The beauty of the framework is that we can relate it back to the psychological reality of our experience.

1. Cognition: Truth

> Sincerity is the end and the beginning of all things; without sincerity there would be nothing.
>
> Confucius

The value associated with Cognition is Truth. The first lesson we have to learn about dealing with the material world is to discover what it is, without illusions or delusions. We have to use our intelligence, our perceptions, our rationality, to see the world as it is. This is what Confucius means when he says that without sincerity there would be nothing – all we would have would be our unsustainable attempts to avoid the truth.

This value is related to ourselves first of all, that we should be honest with ourselves. And then it also refers to our dealings with others, that we should deal with them on the basis of truth as well. This may seem simple, but very often we have reasons to delude ourselves and others. We like to think that things are not so bad or not so good. In truth, they are what they are.

This value, Truth, is the first implication of the prior condition of this conversation: responsibility. To be responsible, we must accept the truth of things, and search actively for what is the truth.

While the value Truth is the core value named for the dimension of Cognition, there is a family of associated values. Prominent among them are: honesty, sincerity, integrity, reasoning, rationality, trustworthiness, competence and curiosity.

"Integrity" is sometimes set apart from values. People say that integrity refers to whether or not you faithfully live up to your espoused values. Integrity does indeed have this special meaning among the values. But we place it in the family of values with Truth, because if truth means to think and speak in alignment with reality, then integrity belongs with them too – it relates to whether our actions are in alignment with the truths we pronounce.

2. Emotion: Peace

> Peace is our natural state of being.
>
> Lao Tzu, *Tao Te Ching*, verse 31

The value associated with Emotion is Peace. Our emotional dimension is constantly active, and a whole spectrum of emotions sits ready to take centre stage in our consciousness. Prompted by external events and incidents or thrown up by the constant activity of the mind, emotions influence our behaviour, our decisions and our actions more strongly than reason. Our rational thoughts may lead us to one conclusion, but our emotions pull us in another direction.

This is why Peace is the defining value of the dimension of Emotion. It is peace of mind that we need in order to be aware of our emotions and see where they would lead us. To exercise peace of mind is to harmonise the power of our passions with what we know via Cognition.

In the language of emotional intelligence, Peace is the self-management of the emotions. This is not repression of the emotions, but the endeavour to ensure that our emotions do not drive us to behaviour that is destructive of ourselves or others. If we see Peace as the self-management of the emotions, this is to say that it takes the ego down from its throne.

When a person is "carried away" by their emotions, it is the ego that is in control, the ego with its self-obsessed desires and its fears. Peace is the result of separating ourselves from the fears and desires that the ego constantly throws at us. It is peace of mind that brings harmony to relationships.

While the value Peace is the core value named for the dimension of Emotion, there is a family of associated values. Prominent among them are: harmony, discipline, humility, cheerfulness, caring, hope, politeness and moderation. Reflecting on all of these associated values gives a fuller idea of what is meant by the core value of this dimension.

3. Moral Valuing: Right Action

> An ethical act is one which does not harm others' experience or expectation of happiness.
>
> Dalai Lama (*Ancient Wisdom, Modern World: Ethics for the new millennium*)

The value associated with Moral Valuing is Right Action. The term "Right Action" is used to sum up what we mean by conduct that reflects what we learn through the dimension of moral valuing. Right Action means we act fairly and justly towards others. We do not cheat, steal, practise deceit, or treat another harshly, and we support Right Action in social contexts – in our organisations, our groups and in society.

Of the five core human values, Right Action is the one that is explicitly concerned with ethical actions. It is explicitly concerned with how our actions contribute to or harm the well-being of others.

Right Action is the core value for Moral Valuing; it stands for a family of associated values. Prominent among them are: fairness, justice, respect, dignity, non-violence, honour, reliability, loyalty, duty, courage, modesty, selflessness, rectitude and correctness. All of these values form part of what is referred to as Right Action. We also include responsibility here. We have said that responsibility is a pre-condition to any discussion of ethics, but it is also particularly associated with Right Action.

4. Spirit: Love

> To love your neighbour as yourself, that is greater than any sacrifice.
>
> Jesus (Mark 12:33)

The value associated with Spirit (or Energy) is Love. The spirit dimension of experience is more than emotions. The spirit dimension is about our connectedness to all-that-is when we are open to what is greater than ourselves, and we are in harmony with ourselves and others. In the diagram, the Spirit dimension overlays the first three dimensions, and so it illustrates how living out the core values of Honesty, Peace and Right Action creates an energy for change.

When a person, a group or an organisation seeks to live out those core values, fundamental human needs are met and trust grows. Commitment to human values becomes conscious and love is possible. In work contexts the word "love" may seem confronting, and perhaps it is better understood in those contexts as deep respect for other people as humans. Other people are seen as more than just a means to fulfil business ends.

The quote from Jesus, which echoes the definition of ethics we have offered earlier, suggests that it is in the Spirit dimension that ethics starts to be truly fulfilled. Ethics is not confined to the Moral Valuing dimension, which looks to the law and social expectations of values like fairness as its measure. In the Spirit dimension, the larger purpose and the deeper meaning of ethics are engaged – we see the deeper meaning of having regard to the well-being of others.

This description explains why the Spirit dimension is distinguished from the Emotion dimension. Without Spirit, the dimension of Emotion can degenerate into sentimentality.

Love is the flag-bearer for a family of values that show its full meaning. They include: compassion, tolerance, enthusiasm, sense of community, friendliness, fun, grace, joy, benevolence, kindness, trust, creativity and reverence.

5. Identity: Insight

His virtue is firm, strong, brilliant.
He corresponds with heaven
And acts in accordance with time.
Thus there is supreme progress and success.

Confucius (commentary on *I Ching* hexagram 14: Ta Yu)

The value associated with Psyche (or Identity) is Insight. What distinguishes this value from the other four core values is that this value can be described as receptive rather than active. Insight is about seeing the whole, seeing how "everything under heaven" makes sense. It is the awareness that it is worthwhile to be virtuous, the knowing that it is only when we act with honesty, seek harmony with people, observe right action and love our neighbour that there will be peace, harmony and prosperity in the world.

In saying that Insight is the value associated with Identity (or Psyche), we are recognising that the development of a person into their fullness as an individual rests on their "living in accordance with heaven". The unique, creative person which is the fulfilled promise of you as "all you can be" must be based on truth, peace, right action, love and insight. This is in opposition to the popular belief that being an individual means pursuing a selfish path and looking after only your own interests.

Note that the life lived in accordance with the core human values being described here is not a life of social conformism. Groups and societies are the expression of a given level of awareness in relation to ethics and human values; they are not perfect. Hence they have blind spots. For example, most societies today reject the idea of slavery, but it has not always been so. In many times and places it

32

has been the accepted thing that some people are entitled to enslave others. To be ethical in this context would require you to step outside the social norms.

To live in accordance with the five core human values, you observe everything in life for yourself and you take responsibility for your own insights. You do not simply conform to what is deemed socially to be correct and acceptable. Thus the value Insight is the value that crystallises your identity as an individual.

The full meaning of the value Insight is embodied in a family of associated values, among them awareness, consciousness, purpose, meaning, appreciation, forgiveness, wisdom, equality, beauty, faith, reverence and equanimity.

Applying the five core human values

This model of the person having five dimensions, each having a core human value, needs to be situated in context so we can see how it can be used in practice. A model is only as good as the use we can make of it. In the next chapter we will look at what is necessary to apply the model to our everyday conduct and experience.

Chapter 6:
Six aims of life and four domains of activity

In the end, each of us will be judged by our standard of life, not by our standard of living, by our measure of giving, not by our measure of wealth, by our simple goodness, not by our seeming greatness.

Hamid Isfahanizadeh (speaker at Metropolis Congress, Sydney, October 2008)

It is one thing to articulate a set of values. It ennobles our spirit to talk of high human values. But values mean nothing if we do not seek to live them. Yet how do we do so? What does it mean to live in accordance with the values of honesty, peace, right action, love and insight?

Four domains

We sometimes speak of humans as consisting of mind, body and spirit. So far we seem to have been talking about mind and spirit, and the body has not been mentioned. It is useful to think of the core human values as being applied in four domains, the first of which is your own body. What binds the core human values together is the notion of ethics as regard for (or care for) the well-being of others. We begin by having regard for the well-being of our own body.

The four domains in which we exist are of two types: physical and social. And for each, there is a "near" domain and a "far" domain. The near domain for the physical is our own body. What is the far domain for the physical? It is all the physical world (both the natural world and the created/built world) around us.

And what are the domains we call social? The near domain for the social is our close personal relationships – family, work teams, friends, while the far domain is the wider social environment – organisations, communities and society.

All of the contexts where we exercise our ethics (or fall short) lie in one of these four domains. Figure 3 shows the person (with his/her five-dimensional modality) as the inner circle located within the four domains.

Figure 3: The person located within the four domains of the world

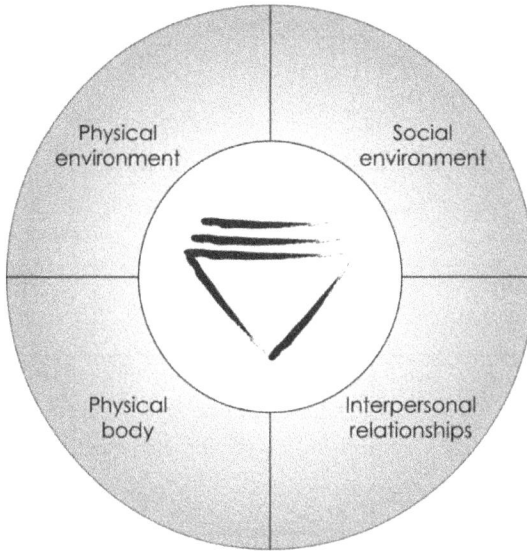

This broader model begins to make sense when we apply it to the question of what our aims are in life. The aims we may have in life are related to what we are trying to do and achieve in the four domains, except that we want to add two further considerations, which apply across all domains.

The two further considerations put a beginning and completion to our aims in life. At the beginning we are helpless babies and our aim is survival – we move towards pleasure and we move away from pain. This is a state of innocence. As we grow, in living our lives we experience the four domains, and for each of them we have key concerns and there is a generic aim for each. Overarching these concerns and aims is another aim that crosses all domains – the concern with the meaning and purpose of our life, which carries the aim of inner peace.

Hence there are six types of aims in life. They are shown in the table below. Of the four domains we have been discussing, we all have our preferences, and each of us is different in where we focus our time and energy. Some of us are primarily concerned about developing intimacy with others (or one other); some of us place our emphasis on adventures in the physical environment. We differ in our emphasis on People or Task, and we differ in our emphasis on "near" or "far" concerns.

Table 1: The aims of life in the four domains

	Domain	Key concerns	Aim
1.	All domains	Survival, pleasure, no pain	Innocence
2.	Physical body	Mastery, independence	Autonomy
3.	Interpersonal relationships	Love	Intimacy
4.	Physical environment	Innovation, adventure, beauty	Harmony, creativity
5.	Social environment	Roles, belonging	Acceptance
6.	All domains	Purpose, meaning	Inner peace

The question this model raises is how we choose what to aim for in life, and whether there is an ethical aspect to this choice. This is a question about which people have different points of view. Some people opt for the focused life, and say that it is important to choose one goal, otherwise your energy will be dissipated among many goals. They say that the people who are successful are the ones who choose one goal and devote all their energy to its achievement.

However, the reality is that we don't do one thing 24 hours a day. If we have a job, then even if the job is very important to us, we go home, and we do other things there, we may have relationships there, we may sing or listen to music, we may restore old furniture. The fact that there are several different domains suggests that there is a need to strike a balance among them. Our fulfilment is actually not about one goal, just as our diet is not about one type of ingredient – we need fruit and vegetables as well as protein.

If the six aims are seen in terms of a general movement, beginning with survival and moving towards purpose, then our fulfilment is about fulfilling aims in all the domains in between. Figure 4 shows the six aims represented as a movement upwards.

Figure 4: The six aims of human life

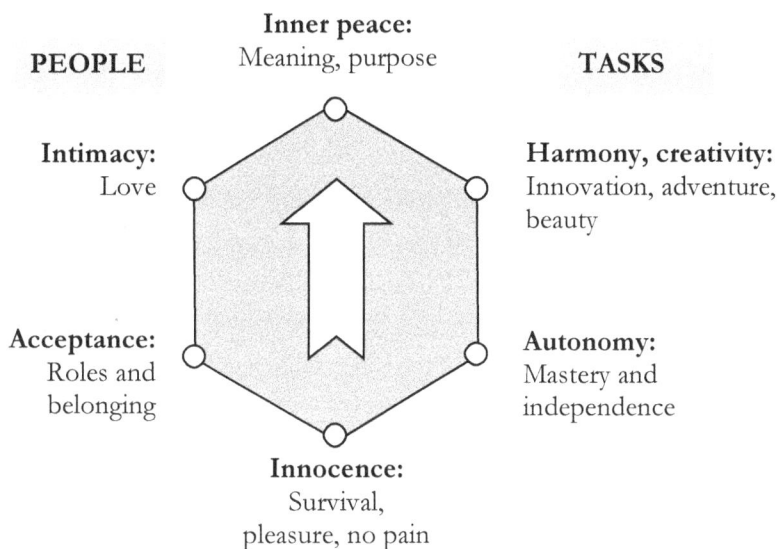

Inner peace:
Meaning, purpose

PEOPLE

TASKS

Intimacy:
Love

Harmony, creativity:
Innovation, adventure,
beauty

Acceptance:
Roles and
belonging

Autonomy:
Mastery and
independence

Innocence:
Survival,
pleasure, no pain

The ethics of choosing aims in life

Is there an ethical aspect to how we choose what to pursue in life? The answer is suggested by what has already been written to this point. We are given much freedom in how we live our lives. Even in environments where our choices are very limited, we have the final freedom of choosing the attitude with which we will live our life. In practice, most of us have a great deal of freedom, and our greatest obstacle is the limitations of our own perception and imagination.

Accordingly, it would seem that our first ethical task is to take responsibility for our own life, and to look at our life and our choices as freely as possible, exercise our imagination, and cultivate an openness to the possibilities. Then, having made choices, taking responsibility for ourselves would suggest that we are prepared to use our best efforts to achieve our aims.

The second ethical aspect is to remember that ethics is always present as a guide for our behaviour (*Moral principle restrains one's behaviour*). Having a goal in life is not a licence to trample on others so that you can attain your goal. The words of the Dalai Lama are pertinent: "Happiness arises from virtuous causes. If we truly desire to be happy, there is no other way to proceed but by way of virtue." He also says, "What brings us greatest joy and satisfaction in life are those actions we undertake out of concern for others."

Exploring the six aims of human life

1. Survival – Pleasure, no pain – Innocence

In the beginning we are innocent and without knowledge of the world or people, helpless. The world may be threatening but it is also a source of wonderment. Life is simple and intense.

What are we trying to do? We try to obtain pleasure and avoid pain. Although this aim is instinctive rather than conscious, it nevertheless directs action. At its most basic, this drive is for survival. This drive incorporates the basic functions that people carry out to both survive and sustain life, from self-protection to eating. It includes all the things we do for enjoyment too.

The pleasure/pain principle does not disappear as people expand their experience – instead, it is placed in a wider perspective. For example, people postpone pleasure in order to complete projects and achieve goals.

The pleasure/pain principle is also applied to a wider range of contexts as we develop. As our knowledge and intellect expand and we acquire ideas about many social activities, we experience new forms of pleasure and pain. Our appreciation of music or visual art depends on the sensibilities we have developed, but pleasure and pain lie at their root. Similarly, we feel pleasure or pain in the emotional realm because of understandings and empathy we have developed. We may, for example, be moved by a person's act of kindness.

The ethical quest for this aim is to discover how we can ensure our survival and pursue pleasure without harming others.

2. The physical body – Mastery, independence – Autonomy

The second type of aim in people's experience is to gain control over themselves, their body and their circumstances. People make a transition from dependence to independence, autonomy and freedom. They gain knowledge and skills and apply them to acquire proficiency in different areas of their lives. They go through many iterations of this process and, indeed, this process never ends.

Looking at this aim as a progression of the child, we see that the child is first content to be dependent and have things done for them by their parents, for example, being carried from place to place. But then the child takes it on as a project to learn to stand and walk, and the aim is to do it for him/herself, even to the point of rejecting the parent's assistance.

This drive extends to more and more spheres of life – learning to read, leaving home, training for an occupation, pursuing a career – all express this drive. As with pleasure/pain, as we develop, this drive extends into different realms. The first realm is physical, mastering one's own body and mind. Later the challenges may be mental and the challenges become more sophisticated. We learn that gaining control is not just about strength but how to handle strength with grace, how to turn our energy towards a goal.

The aim of autonomy extends into spheres such as work, business and relationships. How do we support ourselves financially? What occupational skills do we develop in order to create a sphere in which we are master/mistress? What kind of work situation do we pursue (employee, starting a business etc)? How do we go about establishing and maintaining a home (renting, sharing, buying)? What do we know about finding our way around town?

The key words associated with this aim are mastery, proficiency, capability and freedom. The achievement is to be able to do something and get a desired result with confidence, and to have the opportunity to do this.

The ethical quest for this aim is to discover how we can achieve autonomy while having regard for the well-being of others. For some people, this domain becomes the place where they choose to directly serve the well-being of others.

3. Interpersonal relationships – Love – Intimacy

As well as mastering physical things, the person seeks to experience interpersonal relationships that are mutually satisfying. Intimacy is about establishing a close relationship with an individual or individuals, in contrast to belonging to a group.

Intimacy can be described as the enjoyment of being with another person. This enjoyment has a number of features. It implies closeness, openness and sharing. It involves a willingness to take risks in self-revelation and self-expression, and to be vulnerable. Intimacy involves sharing with another person your thoughts, feelings and values. Part of the risk lies in moving from having *transactions* with a person to having a *relationship* with them. We can describe this as experiencing oneself in relationship to another person.

Intimacy may or may not be physical or sexual. It involves accepting the other person and experiencing that they accept you too – for the whole of what you are, as you are, not merely for some particular traits you have, or for some idealised concept of you. Physical qualities such as beauty may or may not be present, or other qualities such as an engaging personality, valued social role (prestige) or ability to provide goods and services (money, skills and willingness to serve).

The aim of intimacy is to give and receive love. All of the human aims involve the person doing certain things, but in each case the hope is that those actions result in a response. Being intimate involves being open to another, giving of oneself. But one hopes for reciprocity – that the other person knows what you intend and feels the same.

In such delicate country, ethical considerations may assume great intensity. The desire for intimacy may lead to inappropriate efforts to coerce the other person and manipulate their feelings.

4. Physical environment – Innovations, adventure, beauty – Harmony and creativity

After we have mastered ourselves and our environment, a further aim opens up, to develop our skills and knowledge in order to express creativity. The driver may be adventure, innovation or simply beauty.

Creativity is about creating something new and perhaps beautiful, or doing something challenging for its own sake. Of course this can be related back to pleasure and/or mastery, but it seems fit to distinguish it from them. When we ask the question, "What is the person trying to do?", it seems worth noticing that people often do things that have no practical value or need. They do them just for the sake of beauty, challenge or innovation. Music, art and all forms of artistic performance are created and appreciated as ends in themselves.

As this list of human aims expands, the scope for tension between aims becomes evident, particularly from our ethical perspective. Am I neglecting people who rely on me in order to pursue my art? Other ethical questions also arise from the aim of creativity. For example, the integrity of my creative pursuits may be an issue – does my work of art further my creative development and expression or is it an attempt to flatter the audience? Am I lazy in my artistic efforts?

Again, for some people, this domain becomes the place where they choose to directly serve the well-being of others.

5. Social environment – Roles, belonging – Acceptance

This aim is about the person's relationship to other people in a social sense (society, institutions). Having an identity as a member of social groups is a stage of development to adulthood, and it remains highly important for many people. People define themselves as a member of institutions (families, school, other organisations). They understand themselves in terms of a role, which provides a set of norms and activities that structure their existence.

This aim draws on other aims of the person, especially the aim of exercising one's skills and knowledge, but here the focus is on the social effect of the exercise of those powers. The term "expert" refers not just to skills and knowledge (personal mastery), but to the use of them in the service of institutional aims. One is an expert teacher in a school, for example, or an IT expert who can write a program to control air traffic.

The concern to belong leads to the aim of acceptance. The person is trying to get other people to accept them as having a legitimate and valued place in the social web.

There are two ethical questions that this aim raises. The first is: have I fulfilled the obligations of my role (manager, employee, professional, public official etc)? The second question is: is my behaviour ethical in terms of the core human values? The two questions may be in conflict with each other if there is a climate of corruption. There may be an expectation that you act corruptly.

Most of our ethical dilemmas revolve around social roles. When we apply the core human values in context, that context is most often one where you occupy a certain role and there are expectations that are attached to it. You are a doctor, a manager, a bus driver, a teacher, a shop assistant, an electrician. All of these roles carry social expectations, and these social expectations are not always in alignment with what having regard for the well-being of others requires, or what the core human values would seem to require.

6. Purpose – Meaning – Inner peace

The final aim of humans is to come to a position of inner peace about their life. Through an understanding of "who they are" and "what they are here for" they acquire a confidence and awareness about all that happens to and around them. With this understanding comes an aliveness and joy, an acute awareness of their strengths and an acceptance of their limitations.

The aim of understanding one's meaning or purpose is accompanied by a willingness to work with what one has at one's disposal. The daily mechanics of living are not the ceiling of one's experience, but the arena where larger purposes are pursued. Meaning is informed by an appreciation of the finitude of societies, systems and norms.

The emergence of purpose filters through all the other aims, and all the domains. When purpose crystallises, a sense of harmony with all-that-is prevails. The aim of knowing one's purpose, or giving meaning to one's existence, is ever-present and infuses all of a person's actions and endeavours in some way.

The ethical issue posed by this aim is whether we are prepared to put our faith in the meaning we divine for our life. It is fitting to use the word "divine" here. It carries two meanings – first, that we summon greater meaning from life than can be found in the material world, that is, life is in some sense spiritual, and second, that to find our sense of meaning we must plumb our own depths, like diviners looking for water hidden beneath the surface of the earth.

Returning to the five core human values

The core human values speak to how we are constructed as human beings. We are made up of cognition, emotions, moral valuing, spirit and psyche. And we begin with the drive to survive, so our first focus is on our own welfare. But then we realise that we are not the only person in the world. There are others who are like us – we may wish to survive, experience pleasure and avoid pain, but so do they.

In tandem with this realisation, we see that our survival depends on other people. As to the natural world, we learn that our survival depends on it too. We breathe its air, drink its water and eat its food.

From these beginnings, ethics infuses all of the six aims. The choices we make and the way we live our lives rapidly become complex because what is ethical and what is of immediate practical benefit to ourselves do not always coincide. Personal development is therefore about clarifying our choices and firming our resolve to live in an ethical way, knowing ourselves as creatures of the six desires of human life who are learning in every area of our life the deep sense in which it is worthwhile to be ethical.

There is a unifying thread in our complex quest, and that is the desire to find and experience the meaning of our own life, and an understanding of how the world works. We see, as the Dalai Lama says, that we are all intertwined, and my well-being depends on others, and likewise, their well-being depends on me.

Just as we are made of five dimensions, located in four domains, so too we are located in time. We have aims because there are things that we seek to fulfil as we enter into the future, that are not yet complete. This being the case, we need the qualities of patience, perseverance, inner strength and tranquillity.

Our learning is about what the core human values mean in the context of the four domains. When we talk about honesty, peace, right action, love and insight, what do they mean when we are striving to be autonomous, or when we are striving to establish an intimate relationship? Learning is best done by asking these questions constantly. Applying the principles of the core human values rests upon our perceptions of a situation, and for each of us, that perception will be different. Thus it is important to make the distinction between ethical rules that we apply to ourselves and ethical rules that we apply to others. We know our own perceptions and motivations; we can only guess at those of other people.

The *Tao Te Ching* says:

> Those who arrive at their destination
> Teach those who are still on the path,
> While those who are still on the path
> Are sources of wisdom for the teachers.

(Verse 27)

Chapter 7:
Seven levels of consciousness

When the greatness of the Tao is present,
Action rises from one's own heart.
When the greatness of Tao is absent,
Action comes from the rules of 'kindness and justice'.
If you need rules to be kind and just,
If you *act* virtuous,
This is a sure sign that virtue is absent.
Thus we see the great hypocrisy.

    Lao Tzu, *Tao Te Ching*, verse 18 (Wayne Dyer's rendition)

(And what is the 'Tao'? We may call it the supreme reality, or the essence of all-that-is.)

What has been said so far raises the idea that people develop their perception of ethics and their understanding of the world. In fact we began by making the distinction between three orientations towards ethics: Law, Relationships and Identity. We described these as follows:

- **Law:** Ethics is compliance with the laws of society, and the rules of the organisations we belong to. We ask: "What behaviour is required or prohibited by the law or the relevant authority?"
- **Relationships:** Ethics is based on establishing and maintaining deep, trusting relationships with other people. We ask: "Will my actions foster trusting relationships?"
- **Identity:** Ethics is about whether I am living up to my own personal standards. We ask: "Am I living in accordance with the highest values I know?"

We suggested that conversations about ethics often occur because people are talking from the perspective of these different orientations towards ethical obligations. When we look at this aspect more closely, we find that we can identify seven different levels of consciousness, or we could call them world views, and each is associated with a different attitude towards ethics.

To understand how this can be, consider that in relation to the law, there are two different orientations. A person can be resistant to the constraints that the law makes on their actions (a lawless attitude), or they can be accepting and compliant (a law-abiding attitude). And similarly the other two orientations break up into subtler distinctions.

Let's describe this evolution in attitudes, consciousness or world views, starting with lawlessness. We don't have to see these levels in a rigid way and slot people into one or the other of them. People are more fluid than that and they may reflect several of the levels in different situations and at different times. At the same time, one level tends to predominate for a person. There is also a general flow in one direction, an evolution from lower to higher, a tendency to move towards a broader, more inclusive perspective.

Table 2: The evolution of ethical perceptions

LEVEL	ATTITUDE TOWARDS ETHICS
ORIENTATION: LAW	
1 Self-preservation	Ethics is not respected, nor is the law. The focus is on survival of self, and domination of others or annihilation of any perceived threats.
2. Institutional loyalty	Ethics is seen in terms of compliance with laws or organisational policies and norms. Interpretation of rules is literal. Focus is on obedience and conventions.
ORIENTATION: RELATIONSHIPS	
3. Respect for institutions	Ethics is seen in terms of mutual support of family, clan and organisation members. Focus is on competency and effective functioning.

4. Respect for individuals	Ethics is seen in terms of objectivity, social justice, fairness. Focus is on respect for people, not tied to organisational roles.
5. Personal values	Ethics is seen in terms of moral principles that are shared across communities. The focus is on right conduct towards others and ongoing learning and development.
ORIENTATION: IDENTITY	
6. Social collaboration	Ethics is seen in terms of fostering positive change in communities and society. The focus is on collaboration where the self is part of the human family.
7. Global transformation	Ethics is seen as bringing the mystery and possibility of humanity into its fullness. The focus is on social responsibility, service, sustainability and future generations.

If people have these different perceptions of what the world is like, they will take these different attitudes towards ethics. If a person operating out of Level 1 were to have a conversation about ethics with a person operating out of Level 5, it could be a very confused or deceitful conversation. The reason it might be deceitful is that in the public arena, people tend to talk at around Levels 4 and 5. So publicly everyone talks as if we all agreed that we should be truthful, fair, just and respectful towards others. It is expected that we all subscribe to these generally accepted values.

However, a person operating out of Level 1 has no commitment to honesty or fairness. None. If they say they believe in honesty, they are saying it only because it serves their purposes – it is useful for them if you believe what they say.

But we also need to keep in mind that we cannot be definitive about what other people really think. The value of fairness would suggest that we should give people the benefit of the doubt. We can only judge behaviour, not thoughts, and we can only judge behaviour in terms of community standards, such as those enshrined in laws.

Beyond that, we are merely expressing an opinion about behaviour, attempting perhaps to shame someone into acting more kindly, for example.

We are complex creatures. None of us inhabits just one level all of the time. And we change over time, and when we do, it is generally towards a higher level. For a given person at a given time, a particular level will be dominant. This is what can make conversations about ethics so indeterminate. People are arguing out of different perceptions of what the world is like.

If you believe that the world (and hence, other people) is a constant threat, then it makes sense to defeat the threat. If you believe that we are all part of one human family, and that the purpose of life is collaboration with others, then treating people harshly will be seen as inappropriate. This will lead to differences of opinion about what is ethical and what is not. The Level 1 attitude of self-preservation will see the Level 6 attitude of social collaboration, not as ethical, but as completely unrealistic.

This brings us to the quote at the beginning of the chapter. The writer, Lao Tzu, accepts the value of kindness and justice, but observes that this is but an interim position in the great scheme of things, it is not the most desirable state. When we have to make it a rule to be kind and just, we are not expressing what is ideal. The ideal is that we are kind and just out of our very nature, not as an act that we put on.

The seven levels of consciousness are stages on the journey towards the realisation of what we might call the mystery and possibility of being human. The true meaning of ethics is the full realisation of what it means to have regard for the well-being of others and to restrain the drive of the ego to serve only its own ends. Along the way we try to regulate ourselves, and in societies we establish rules and norms and laws, and so we may "act" virtuously, but as the writer Lao Tzu says, as admirable as this may be, in the end it is still hypocrisy. The ideal is to do what is right intuitively and spontaneously.

We should say again that the model is neater than reality. In reality we find that our thinking over a particular period of time is dominated by one level of consciousness, but on occasion we inhabit a lower level or we see to a higher level. Our lives are a dynamic process. Over time we may find that our world view has shifted, and the new consciousness becomes stable. Accordingly our views on ethics evolve.

And what does it mean for us, that there are these different levels of consciousness, or world views? Does it mean that we are prisoners of a particular perspective, or that our shortcomings are excused? No. Our task is just this: to seek to raise the level of our consciousness each day. This might sound grand, but all it means is that we seek to see our circumstances from a broader, more inclusive, less selfish perspective. We seek to see the deeper, longer-term workings of the world.

The impetus for this quest is that we are at a point in the history of our world where the actions of humanity have greater effect on the future of the world than they have ever had. We have extraordinary powers at our disposal through technology. If we do not begin to live lives that are more in harmony with the earth, our future looks bleak. And in terms of our personal and collective experience, if we do not begin to see beyond more and more rampant consumerism, we will drive ourselves into the emptiness of despair.

It is precisely the voice of ethics that is needed to counter this stampede into the oblivion of consumption and self-obsession. To live ethically is to live from the whole, to live with the well-being of all in mind. There is an ancient eastern saying: "I am not, but the universe is myself". The ego initially gives us our sense of individuality, our uniqueness and importance, but unless it is absorbed into the larger vision of all-that-is, where we all have an equal right to exist, it leads us to trample on others in the mistaken belief that this is how to get our needs met.

The vision that becomes clear at Level 7 in the above model is that we best get our real (spirit) needs met when we take account of the needs of all, recognising that we are no different in essence from others.

Live with the whole in mind.

Seek to raise the level of your consciousness each day.

Chapter 8:
Practice – living ethically

We are what we repeatedly do.

Aristotle

The wise person, the noble one, *junzi*, has the ability to judge what is the right thing to do in a given situation.

Confucius

To live ethically is to live in harmony. How is this so? It is so because to live ethically is to live with regard for the well-being of others. When I live only to serve myself, others exist only as a means to my ends. But the self is alone in this; it is an attitude that puts others at a distance and diminishes them. When the "I" gives way to consideration for others, and we live with compassion and thoughtfulness, we see others as whole persons, and the self is liberated to enter into community with others.

The beginning of the ethical life is awareness of the self, opening our thoughts, words and actions to examination. We apply the dimension of moral valuing to evaluate them. And we resolve to accept responsibility for who we are and what we do, and for our effect on others.

This all sounds right and proper, but our experience is frequently not so positive. We try to do good and we are rewarded with trouble, opposition and grief. We try to do good and others take advantage of us. It seems difficult to be ethical, and we wonder, is it really worthwhile?

Even when we resolve to be ethical, we frequently fall short of our own standards. We do and say things that we regret. How are we to come back and try again?

These are the issues we face when we try to live ethically. That is why the chapter title contains the word "practice". The word can be understood in two senses. Firstly, it means that living ethically takes practice. We don't always "get it right" but if we keep "practising" we will get better at it.

Secondly, practice means that living ethically is pursued as a regular habit, exercise or discipline. It is how we live, it is something that we do consciously and constantly. Ethics is not primarily a philosophical argument about propositions, logic and justifications. It is an attitude towards life that we put into practice, and in the approach described in this book, it is about how we live with regard for the well-being of others.

Steps in the practice of living ethically

It would be silly to think that the practice of living ethically could be reduced to a simple checklist. There are steps to take, but they are not steps that can be taken glibly, and our experience will tell us that we need to keep coming back to the beginning, back to all the steps, continually. The things that have been discussed here are basic themes for the ethical life. The steps described below are to be understood from this perspective.

Step 1: Take responsibility for your life.

Responsibility means that you accept responsibility for your thoughts, words, and actions, and you hold yourself accountable for them. Looking back, we recognise any wrongdoing we have done or harm we have caused, and we accept any punishment and make whatever recompense we can for harm caused. Looking forward, we undertake not to act in the same way again.

We recognise the influences and pressures on us, from our peer group, organisational norms, or from our upbringing or natural inclinations, that led to our actions. We recognise any fears or desires that drive us. But we accept that ultimately it is we ourselves who choose how we act.

Step 2: Commit to personal moral principles.

Each of these steps unfolds from the previous step. Once we take responsibility for our life, the next step is to make a commitment to personal moral principles. This is to say that we think about ethics for ourselves; we do not simply follow our social group's norms, whether that is our family, our employer, our church or any other organisation we belong to. We each see the world uniquely, and this means that we each see ethical issues in our own unique way. Committing to moral principles means that we set the intention to live up to the ethical standards that present themselves to us.

Another way of saying this is that we commit to listening to the voice of our conscience, we commit to educating and developing our conscience, and we accept the responsibility of making our own judgements. We do not simply accept what others say or do without question.

Step 3: Cultivate awareness of yourself.

Cultivating awareness of the self means recognising our internal environment that leads to our words and behaviour. As Figure 1 in Chapter 5 showed, our words and actions are a product of our thoughts, emotions, moods, needs, interests, attitudes, concerns and values. If our words and actions cause us shame, it is there that we must look.

None of what lies within us is unchangeable. As we become more aware of the current dynamics of our mind, we can shift to what is more satisfying and harmonious, knowing that the key is to restrain the ego by cultivating a concern for the well-being of others, and by keeping the whole in mind (the well-being of all-that-is) rather than narrowing our focus to short-term, selfish gain.

There are many aspects to this practice, and below we will explore the core human values as a way of doing this.

Step 4: Commit to learning and development.

As we experience life we are continually learning. But it is only when this learning is conscious that it can lead us in a positive direction. Otherwise our learning is accidental, and experience will generally only serve to cement us in our current perceptions, attitudes and mental models, whatever they may be at the time. Conscious learning enables us to see our weaknesses and build our strengths, and to chart the direction in which we would like to go.

The essence of learning is questions. We enquire into a subject to find out facts and principles, we enquire into our experience in order to work out how to apply the facts and principles, we monitor our attempts to put new learning into practice, and we enquire again to see how we have performed, and how to improve our performance. Questions require us to pay attention, to think about the meaning of things, to think about how things work, to continually assess what we do against our mental framework and standards, and to reflect on what we have done.

In relation to the ethics of our conduct, we might ask: What makes me clear and strong so that I act ethically? What makes me uncomfortable? What am I discovering? What ideas of mine are being challenged? What moods and other factors affect my actions? What do I not understand about other people? Do I model what I say? What am I learning about myself?

The perspective that "I am a learner" admits that we will make mistakes – learners do, otherwise they are probably not learning anything new. So we will need to forgive ourselves, maybe frequently. But as learners we resolve not to keep making the same mistakes – as we learn, we make new and better ones! And we remember Step 1, that we always take responsibility for our mistakes.

Step 5: Deal with discouragement.

It often seems that when we start paying attention to something, things get worse rather than better. We resolve that we will act ethically in a situation, and rather than thank us and come around to our viewpoint, the people involved attack us. They might even turn around and accuse us of being unethical. These adverse events may discourage us and lead us to question our faith in living ethically.

There is a legitimate question in such circumstances, and that is, am I operating out of my ego? Is my ego telling me that I am more ethical than others, and is this getting in the way of establishing ethical conduct in the situation? You must renew your focus on the goal, which is the well-being of all as the social objective, one that has nothing to do with you personally or anyone else in the situation personally.

There is certainly a need to develop skills to be the voice for values in situations. You need to be articulate, you need clarity, you need confidence, even fearlessness.

And sometimes, it may seem that you have lost. Is this a blow against justice, fairness or kindness in the world? Does it mean that your efforts for ethics have not been worth it? The insight that comes from many religions is that the good intention is never lost, and we should not become too attached to any particular result, favourable or adverse.

We should know, too, that discouragement means to lose courage. One of the defining features of ethics is being able to exercise courage in taking right action.

The important thing in adversity is our ethical intention and our deep commitment to it; there is truth in it that has power that does not die. Because everything is connected and our thoughts have power, spiritual intention works beneath the surface of events in ways that we cannot know. Accordingly, allow your humble and persistent efforts to be ethical to be a deep, authentic part of who you are. In the end, would you want to be anything less?

The core human values seen through the seven levels of consciousness

The concept of seven levels of consciousness indicates that there are seven different ways of viewing ethics. This is a framework that enables us to see how we can grow and develop a broader, more inclusive perspective on life.

In the social arena, people generally talk about basic values such as honesty, fairness, respect, justice and kindness, which we can align with Levels 4 and 5. We can imagine another society where the predominant concepts are harsher and more rigid, and we could say this society operates at Level 2 or 3. And we can imagine an enlightened society where people seek to realise global harmony, and say this is a Level 6 or 7 society.

In our society or organisation, we can seek to encourage a better outlook on ethics. We can speak of kindness and compassion, for example, rather than confining talk to what laws or policies demand. But of its nature, high ethical values have to be voluntary. They have to be the free choice of the individual or the organisation. Having said this, there is no harm in a society demanding a higher level of conduct from organisations. This is simply to say that society expects organisations to treat people, and the environment, decently and with respect.

The view of ethics presented in this book sees ethics as being reflected in each of the five dimensions of the person. We want to revisit these five dimensions and see what they look like from the perspective of each of the seven levels of consciousness, or world views. Doing this gives us a comprehensive account of ethics and the different ways in which people see it.

The quest? To seek to raise the level of our consciousness each day.

1. TRUTH: the value associated with COGNITION

The cognitive dimension of the person has the core value of Truth. Other values that are associated with it include:

- honesty
- integrity
- reasoning
- curiosity
- trustworthiness
- impartiality
- rationality
- competence
- sincerity
- systems thinking

We need to be alert to our tendency to subscribe to one world view verbally (what we espouse) but in practice to act out of another. Adopting the perspective of people who observe our behaviour is one way of disentangling the two: ask, what would other people say about my behaviour? Consider how the truth is seen under the various world views, as described below. Which one explains your behaviour, as it is, most accurately?

World view 1: The truth is treated expediently. Whatever serves the person's survival ends is what is said and done.

World view 2: The truth is treated selectively, that is, whatever serves the interests of the person and their family and friends is what is said and done.

World view 3: The truth is honoured but is filtered through the institutional perspectives that constitute the person's reference groups. The understanding of truth tends to be literal.

World view 4: The truth is pursued in a principled way rather than in a passive or doctrinaire way; this may lead to some conflicts between the person's viewpoint and the institution's.

World view 5: Truth and reality are seen from an expanded perspective, as holistic, incorporating many different dynamics and perspectives, e.g. social, political.

World view 6: Truth merges with peace and love. They are no longer seen as separate; they no longer appear to be in tension with each other.

World view 7: Truth is seen from an inner perspective, where external (material) reality is seen as the expression of the inner truth of the universe and all-that-is.

2. PEACE: the value associated with EMOTIONS

The emotional dimension of the person has the core value of Peace. Other values that are associated with it include:

• caring	• cheerfulness	• affection
• courtesy	• dignity	• humility
• hope	• politeness	• discipline
• harmony	• humility	• moderation

Consider how peace is seen under the various world views, as described below. Again, ask which of the world views explains our behaviour, as it is, most accurately? In doing this, we should pay close attention to the reasons (or justifications) we give ourselves for our behaviour – the object of this exercise is not to deny or invalidate those reasons, but to be sympathetically aware of them.

World view 1: Values directed towards peace (e.g. caring, cheerfulness, politeness) are treated expediently.

World view 2: Values directed towards peace are similarly employed selectively, favouring the security of family and friends.

World view 3: Values directed towards peace are fulfilled in a way that is consistent with the person's commitment to family, authority and institutions.

World view 4: Values directed towards peace are incorporated into enlarged personal goals, in tension at times with other principles, e.g. when injustice occurs.

World view 5: The person pursues peace as a way of exemplifying the better world they are trying to create.

World view 6: The person has a deeper understanding of how peace and all the other values serve the world purpose.

World view 7: Peaceful action proceeds from insight and a sense of the oneness of all things.

3. RIGHT ACTION: the value associated with MORAL VALUING

The moral valuing dimension of the person has the core value of Right Action. Valuing means using our powers of discrimination to assess actions as right or wrong, good or bad – in all the gradations that may apply, not in a simplistic, black-and-white way. Right Action means taking the action that furthers good over bad, or right over wrong, both in terms of our objectives and the means we employ to pursue those objectives, and understanding that good is defined in terms of whether our action has regard for the well-being of others. Right Action manifests through the associated values of:

• duty	• respect	• fairness
• justice	• courage	• reliability
• responsibility	• non-violence	• moderation
• honour	• dignity	• competence
• loyalty	• duty	• modesty
• selflessness	• rectitude	• correctness

To address the above questions for the dimension of Right Action, we need to be aware that sensitivity about our moral conduct reflects back on emotions and cognition – we tend to have strong emotions when an ethical value is at stake, and our cognitive processes work their hardest when they are trying to sustain our sense of self-esteem under ethical pressure. As was said above, the aim here is to bring our conduct into awareness and understand it, not to deny it, justify it or congratulate ourselves.

World view 1: Right action (e.g. duty, respect, fairness, responsibility) is regarded with expediency.

World view 2: Right action extends only to a select group of family and friends.

World view 3: Right action is pursued as a duty in the context of family, institutions and accepted authorities.

World view 4: Right action is pursued passionately but more from an independent perspective than as an unreflective member of an organisation or society.

World view 5: Right action is pursued as the foundation and pre-requisite of human creativity and joy.

World view 6: The person has a deeper understanding of how right action serves the world purpose.

World view 7: Right action is transformed to insight and oneness.

4. LOVE: the value associated with ENERGY/SPIRIT

The energy/spirit dimension of the person has the core value of Love. Love is admitted uncomfortably into the conversation when we are talking about work and organisations. However, when identified through its associated values then its appropriateness, indeed, its necessity, becomes evident:

- enthusiasm
- tolerance
- compassion
- persistence

- sincerity
- sense of community
- friendship
- service

- patience
- collaboration
- fun
- grace

- joy
- trust
- benevolence
- creativity
- kindness

This list of values reveals that the energy for activities in organisations, without which nothing happens and no good ideas come to fruition, comes from love. In organisational contexts the term "deep respect" may be used instead, understanding that it amounts to the same thing. This love can be manifested in the enthusiasm with which people work for the shared goals of the organisation, and the consideration they give to each other.

Applying the questions above to the energy/spirit dimension requires us to examine how the best and the worst can both occur, and what it means for ethics.

World view 1: Values exemplifying love (e.g. friendship, sincerity, patience) are regarded with expediency.

World view 2: Values exemplifying love extend only to a select group of family and friends.

World view 3: Love is exercised as an aspect of belonging to and being part of family, organisations and institutions. It is conditioned by fears about the world, which may intrude into the person's close circle of friends and colleagues.

World view 4: Love is exercised through the recognition of others as individuals and there is a blossoming of compassion and tolerance.

World view 5: Love is exercised from a sense of the connections between people and the possibilities for community across social and political divides.

World view 6: A greater sense of unity is conveyed to others. The person imparts an understanding of inter-connectedness, the need of individuals and communities for each other.

World view 7: Love expressed is palpable and transforming.

5. INSIGHT: the value associated with IDENTITY/PSYCHE

The identity/psyche dimension is the one that takes us into ourselves most deeply, to discover our personal purpose and meaning, hence its core value is Insight. Insight is explained more fully through its associated values of:

- appreciation
- meaning
- equality
- purpose
- faith
- awareness
- consideration
- beauty
- consciousness
- equanimity
- forgiveness
- wisdom
- reverence

At this point we need to be most alert with ourselves, remembering that social desirability leads us all to attest to high personal values. But we have to work with who we really are right now, not some fond illusion. Some bravery is required to admit what is evident by our conduct and our priorities.

Again, explore the above questions with the confidence that you know more about yourself than you may like to admit. Examine your reactions to incidents at work and what your conduct says about your beliefs.

World view 1: Not applicable.

World view 2: Not applicable.

World view 3: The meaning of reality is understood in terms of social structures, institutions and traditions.

World view 4: Awareness is seen as personal, unshackled from institutional perspectives, although this may be accompanied by trepidation.

World view 5: Insight begins to assume power, informed by an appreciation of the world and by the integration of the value dimensions of truth, peace, right action and love.

World view 6: Forgiveness, compassion, equality and wisdom come to the fore as the systemic, inter-connected nature of reality becomes clearer.

World view 7: The place of everyone and everything in the overall scheme of things infuses all perceptions and actions: "Humanity's natural state is bliss."

Review and application

Working regularly and actively with this framework will deepen your understanding of what motivates you, and other people, to act ethically or otherwise. It will increase your understanding of yourself and enable you to develop your skills to act both ethically and effectively in business and organisational contexts. You will increasingly be clearer about what is ethical and be confident in following that path, regardless of whether you have to act alone or are supported.

The key concept in the outworking of values in our lives is the ongoing subjection of our conduct to the five core human values. All actions reflect values in some way and the values invest actions with meaning. The caution that is needed in tackling specific actions is that actions can convey different meanings to different people, and multiple values can arise out of one action. For example, promptness in ending a meeting may express efficiency; it may also occur at the expense of addressing an important issue or allowing a person to express their views.

The lesson is that in addressing specific actions and how they reflect or embody values, we must keep in mind the overall set of values and exercise judgement. We need to articulate the values at stake and be imaginative in how we find a solution that satisfies the overall set of values. In the example mentioned, we might extend the meeting if we have obtained the group's consent, or find another way to satisfy the human values at stake here, perhaps by scheduling another group meeting or continuing the meeting by email.

The ongoing work of bringing values to expression involves moving backwards and forwards between the articulation of values (talk) and interpretation of them in practice (action). This continual process of interpretation, practice and review leads to the internalisation of principles, and results in improved decision-making skills. This is depicted in Figure 5.

Figure 5: The relationship between values and practice

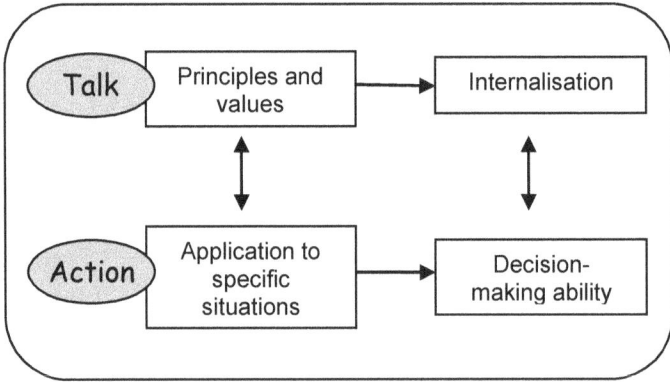

Roles and relationships

It is worth making some specific observations about roles and relationships. Just about all of our actions take place in social contexts and affect or are affected by others. It is no accident that the five dimensions of the person are capped by the dimensions of spirit and psyche, and that their core values are love, harmony and insight into the oneness of all things. This perspective emphasises the importance of relationships in the structure of reality.

There are many kinds of relationships in societies. Many of these are hierarchical – child-parent, student-teacher, employer-employee, worker-manager, follower-leader. Some are horizontal – brothers, sisters, fellow workers, peers. All of the human values apply to these relationships, of course, but often they have to be interpreted against a context of power and influence.

There is nothing in the core human values approach that rejects the existence of hierarchies. There is no suggestion, for example, that "equality" is possible or even desirable between child and parent. An objective view of the structure of the situation would suggest that the parent has knowledge, skills, resources and emotional maturity that the child does not have, and the parent should exercise authority, appropriately. What the core human values would suggest is that authority should be exercised in accordance with the values of honesty, peace, right action, love and insight.

What that means in practice is up for discussion and learning from experience in particular contexts. Ethics is not about abstract rules and principles; it is about the meaning of our actions in particular contexts, with all the richness and complexity that that implies.

The core human values perspective highlights the fact that ethics requires a balanced approach, through an active consideration of all the values. Good parenthood, or the aspiration to ethical conduct in any sphere, is not just about one aspect.

Similar things can be said about relationships in organisations. What is of even more importance there is to respect the fact that employees are adults. There is a tendency in many organisations for managers to adopt parent-child stances towards employees rather than adult-adult.

Another observation is that the ethical leader always fosters development. Our conduct as the more powerful person in a relationship is not just about maintaining the current status. A healthy relationship is about how we can develop it further.

In an organisation, for example, the current state of decision-making may involve little or no consultation with employees. This is generally so for historical reasons, that is, it may have always been that way. But an ethical leader will be asking, how can we develop so that decision-making is more respectful of the workforce? How can employees be consulted and participate in the future direction and strategies of the organisation?

Linking the core human values and the five elements in Chinese philosophy

The five core human values can be readily associated with the five elements of Chinese philosophy – earth, water, metal, fire and wood. This can be helpful in deepening our understanding of the core human values. The table shows the correspondence between the elements and the values.

Table 3: The five Chinese elements and core human values

Dimension	Core value	Element
Cognition	Truth	Earth
Emotions	Peace	Water
Moral Valuing	Right Action	Metal
Energy/Spirit	Love	Fire
Identity/Psyche	Insight	Wood

A description of the association between each element and value follows.

Cognition: Earth

Cognition deals with "concrete" facts about situations and involves logic and reasoning. It links to earth, representing the raw material with which we work in life.

Emotions: Water

Emotions deal with people's feelings and attitudes. They link to water, evoking the flow of emotions in our experience and the quality of both water and emotions to adapt in response to the context in which they find themselves.

Valuing: Metal

Valuing concerns the exercise of judgement about what is right and wrong, and following through with right action. Metal evokes the image of a sword dividing left from right. Or we think of a set of scales made of metal, that weighs up two things and compares them. Metal artifacts are made with precision and care, evoking clarity and discernment. Metal has a strong association with earth, but it is distinguished from it, reminding us that moral valuing is not just a question of assessing facts. Likewise metal is distinct from water, reminding us that valuing can be an emotional activity but it is not reducible to feelings.

Energy: Fire

Energy is about the power that is released when people are in harmony with the human values of truth, peace and right action, a power that is an expression of love or grace. Likewise, fire is released when the right conditions are in place, bringing warmth and light and joy.

Identity: Wood

Identity is about the awareness of one's self and purpose, and feeling in tune with one's purpose. This insight evokes the image of wood, which represents the tree, the single element which is living and organic. The tree exists and thrives in the presence of the other elements, and it is the fulfilment of their potentiality. It is expansive, nurturing, versatile, and growing.

Integrating the five core human values

The imagery of the five Chinese elements is a way of bringing life to the core human values. These images can be used as a meditation to deepen our sensitivity to their unique qualities. By deepening our understanding of them, we help to integrate them into our life, and we see more and more how to apply them in our conduct.

The five core human values can be used to take yourself on a conscious journey of development and improvement. The following statement raises the challenges presented by each of the five dimensions of the person:

> People tend to live in the mechanical (rational, cognitive, routine), are dominated by the emotional (which drives their conduct) and rarely question their values. They tend not to be open to energy/spirit and therefore do not realise their identity. In the face of this inertia, we should:

- question the mechanical/routine
- open ourselves to the emotional
- clarify our values and live them courageously
- welcome the flow of spirit/energy
- discover our psyche/identity.

However, despite the momentum of unconsciousness, we should remember that we are also motivated to seek to become all that we may be. The drive to find meaning and purpose in our lives is strong – it is the living tree, the wood, among the elements of earth, water, metal and fire.

Growing and developing ethically has parallels with becoming an expert in other areas of life. Experts increase their knowledge and effectiveness in many ways, and we can apply similar methods to increase our strengths in living ethically:

- Look for patterns in situations that others do not notice.
- Detect anomalies (eg things that should have happened but didn't) that indicate something is amiss.
- Place actions in a larger framework (the whole system) and understand how things operate, the hidden processes.
- Look for opportunities to take effective action, including improvisations.
- Perceive the flow of events, so that you can see the direction in which things are headed.
- Understand your own limitations.

The core human values are available to all of us, to apply in our situation as we are and where we are. The meaning of the core human values expands as we focus on them and seek to live in accord with them. Through experience, our skills and insight develop and our view of the world undergoes evolution.

Summary of the core human values

Cognition	Emotions	Moral Valuing	Energy/ Spirit	Identity/ Psyche
Truth	Peace	Right Action	Love	Insight
Earth	Water	Metal	Fire	Wood
Honesty	Harmony	Responsibility	Compassion	Awareness
Integrity	Cheerfulness	Respect	Tolerance	Consciousness
Reasoning	Humility	Fairness	Enthusiasm	Purpose
Sincerity	Hope	Justice	Sense of community	Meaning
Trustworthiness	Politeness	Dignity	Friendliness	Appreciation
Competence	Discipline	Courage	Fun	Forgiveness
Curiosity	Patience	Honour	Grace	Wisdom
	Self-discipline	Non-violence	Joy	Equality
	Caring	Reliability	Benevolence	Beauty
	Moderation	Loyalty	Kindness	Faith
		Duty	Trust	Reverence
		Modesty	Creativity	Equanimity
		Selflessness		
		Rectitude		
		Correctness		

A self-awareness exercise

This is an exercise to help you to think about your current orientation towards ethics. It is not intended to be "hard science". It is just a device for helping you to see yourself more clearly and to think about what you are like and what you would like to change.

Consider your current experiences of ethical situations in the light of the descriptions of the core human values under each world view. You will probably find that you typify different perspectives at different times. But how much? Imagine you have 100 points, and you distribute them across the world views according to how much each represents your behaviour. The table that follows gives an example, followed by a narrative description of this person.

On the pages that follow, each table is for one dimension, and your task is to:

> Distribute 100 points across the world views according to how you see your orientation towards ethics at the moment.

There are some questions following the table for each dimension. Use these questions to ponder how you see ethics and how you would like to develop.

SAMPLE RESPONSE (with the dimension Cognition)

Dimension 1: Cognition Core Values: Truth, Honesty, Integrity	
Perception under each World View	**Points**
World view 1: The truth is treated expediently. Whatever serves the person's survival ends is what is said and done.	0
World view 2: The truth is treated selectively, that is, whatever serves the interests of the person and their family and friends is what is said and done.	5
World view 3: The truth is honoured but is filtered through the institutional perspectives that constitute the person's reference groups. The understanding of truth tends to be literal.	25
World view 4: The truth is pursued in a principled way rather than in a passive or doctrinaire way; this may lead to some conflicts between the person's viewpoint and the institution's.	50
World view 5: Truth and reality are seen from an expanded perspective, as holistic, incorporating many different dynamics and perspectives, e.g. social, political.	20
World view 6: Truth merges with peace and love. They are no longer seen as separate; they no longer appear to be in tension with each other.	0
World view 7: Truth is seen from an inner perspective, where external (material) reality is seen as the expression of the inner truth of the universe and all-that-is.	0
TOTAL POINTS	100

Personal comments (for this imaginary person): I have a commitment to honesty, so I wouldn't lie or cheat just to win, or to beat someone (world view 1). I am not so spiritual that I think I see the inner truth of everything (7), or see truth merging with peace and love (6). Most of the time I align with world view 4 – I uphold truth in a principled way, even if it causes difficulties sometimes. Often I tend to accept the organisation's perspective too readily (3), but at times I see that truth is complex and can be seen from different standpoints (5).

MY SELF-AWARENESS EXERCISE

For each of the five tables, allocate 100 points across the seven world views

Dimension 1: Cognition Core Values: Truth, Honesty, Integrity	
Perception under each World View	**Points**
World view 1: The truth is treated expediently. Whatever serves the person's survival ends is what is said and done.	
World view 2: The truth is treated selectively, that is, whatever serves the interests of the person and their family and friends is what is said and done.	
World view 3: The truth is honoured but is filtered through the institutional perspectives that constitute the person's reference groups. The understanding of truth tends to be literal.	
World view 4: The truth is pursued in a principled way rather than in a passive or doctrinaire way; this may lead to some conflicts between the person's viewpoint and the institution's.	
World view 5: Truth and reality are seen from an expanded perspective, as holistic, incorporating many different dynamics and perspectives, e.g. social, political.	
World view 6: Truth merges with peace and love. They are no longer seen as separate; they no longer appear to be in tension with each other.	
World view 7: Truth is seen from an inner perspective, where external (material) reality is seen as the expression of the inner truth of the universe and all-that-is.	
TOTAL POINTS	100

Your comments:

Personal exploration: TRUTH

1. Describe a situation you have experienced where it was difficult to fulfil your personal standards for this value. (This may have been a moral victory, or you may have fallen short of your own values.)

2. For this value, what is a reasonable vision for you to target at this time? Which world view best describes this vision?

Dimension 2: Emotion Core Values: Peace, harmony	
Perception under each World View	**Points**
World view 1: Values directed towards peace (e.g. caring, cheerfulness, politeness) are treated expediently.	
World view 2: Values directed towards peace are similarly employed selectively.	
World view 3: Values directed towards peace are fulfilled in a way that is consistent with the person's commitment to family, authority and institutions.	
World view 4: Values directed towards peace are incorporated into enlarged personal goals, in tension at times with other principles, e.g. when injustice occurs.	
World view 5: The person pursues peace as a way of exemplifying the better world they are trying to create.	
World view 6: The person has a deeper understanding of how peace and all the other values serve the world purpose.	
World view 7: Peaceful action proceeds from insight and a sense of the oneness of all things.	
TOTAL POINTS	100

Your comments:

Personal exploration: PEACE

1. Describe a situation you have experienced where it was difficult to fulfil your personal standards for this value. (This may have been a moral victory, or you may have fallen short of your own values.)

2. For this value, what is a reasonable vision for you to target at this time? Which world view best describes this vision?

Dimension 3: Moral Valuing Core Values: Right Action, Fairness	
Perception under each World View	Points
World view 1: Right action (e.g. duty, respect, fairness, responsibility) is regarded with expediency.	
World view 2: Right action extends only to a select group of family and friends.	
World view 3: Right action is pursued as a duty in the context of family, institutions and accepted authorities.	
World view 4: Right action is pursued passionately but more from an independent perspective than as an unreflective agent of an organisation.	
World view 5: Right action is pursued as the foundation and pre-requisite of human creativity and joy.	
World view 6: The person has a deeper understanding of how right action serves the world purpose.	
World view 7: Right action is transformed to insight and oneness.	
TOTAL POINTS	100

Your comments:

Personal exploration: RIGHT ACTION

1. Describe a situation you have experienced where it was difficult to fulfil your personal standards for this value. (This may have been a moral victory, or you may have fallen short of your own values.)

2. For this value, what is a reasonable vision for you to target at this time? Which world view best describes this vision?

Dimension 4: Energy/Spirit Core Values: Love, Kindness, Joy	
Perception under each World View	Points
World view 1: Values exemplifying love (e.g. friendship, sincerity, patience) are regarded with expediency.	
World view 2: Values exemplifying love extend only to the select group of family and friends.	
World view 3: Love is exercised as an aspect of belonging to and being part of family, organisations and institutions. It is conditioned by fears about the world, which may intrude into the person's close circle of friends and colleagues.	
World view 4: Love is exercised through the recognition of others as individuals and there is a blossoming of compassion and tolerance.	
World view 5: Love is exercised from a sense of the connections between people and the possibilities for community across social and political divides.	
World view 6: A greater sense of unity is conveyed to others. The person imparts an understanding of inter-connectedness, the need of individuals and communities for each other.	
World view 7: Love expressed is palpable and transforming.	
TOTAL POINTS	100

Your comments:

Personal exploration: ENERGY/SPIRIT

1. Describe a situation you have experienced where it was difficult to fulfil your personal standards for this value. (This may have been a moral victory, or you may have fallen short of your own values.)

2. For this value, what is a reasonable vision for you to target at this time? Which world view best describes this vision?

Dimension 5: Identity/Psyche Core Values: Insight, Meaning	
Perception under each World View	**Points**
World view 1: Not applicable.	
World view 2: Not applicable.	
World view 3: The meaning of reality is understood in terms of social structures, institutions and traditions.	
World view 4: Awareness is seen as personal, unshackled from institutional perspectives, although this may be accompanied by trepidation.	
World view 5: Insight begins to assume power, informed by an appreciation of the world and by the integration of the value-dimensions of truth, peace, right action and love.	
World view 6: Forgiveness, compassion, equality and wisdom come to the fore as the systemic nature of reality becomes clearer.	
World view 7: The place of everyone and everything in the overall scheme of things infuses all perceptions and actions: "Humanity's natural state is bliss."	
TOTAL POINTS	100

Your comments:

Personal exploration: IDENTITY/PSYCHE

1. Describe a situation you have experienced where it was difficult to fulfil your personal standards for this value. (This may have been a moral victory, or you may have fallen short of your own values.)

2. For this value, what is a reasonable vision for you to target at this time? Which world view best describes this vision?

Frequently Asked Questions (FAQs)

Q 1. Aren't some things just wrong, like killing or stealing?

We simply need to be aware of what we mean by our statements. When I say that acts such as killing and stealing are wrong, I could mean a number of things. I might mean no more than that I think such acts are wrong, which is to say that I haven't thought about why this might be so. Then, our society asserts that it considers such acts to be wrong and it demonstrates this by establishing laws to punish people who carry out such acts. And Christians believe that killing and stealing are wrong because the Ten Commandments in the Bible say so.

How are we to regard these different grounds for the assertion that certain acts are wrong? We need to be clear about the kind of assertions we are making, otherwise our conversations will become confused. It is not helpful to base our assertions in the external, natural world. Human values, such as respect for the life of other humans or their property, are not self-evident there. If someone is killed or their property is stolen, in terms of the natural world, this is all simply stuff that happens. The world will go on regardless. The sun will still come up in the morning.

So human values are our product, as humans; we create our values and articulate them. Now, religious believers will say the values come from God, via their holy texts. People who do not subscribe to a religious belief may say the values are an inherent aspect of humans, or that the values are necessary for human communities to sustain themselves. A spiritual perspective might say that values are the expression of our yearning for spirit in the midst of the material world – it is the way that heaven mingles with earth.

In any conversation about ethics these diverse perspectives may be represented. There may be agreement about many values, but even then, the reasons may differ. What does this mean? That there is no solid, common ground for the assertion that killing and stealing are wrong?

This takes us back to Chapter 1, where it was said that ethics in social contexts is the result of agreements reached between people, perhaps for a variety of reasons. It was also said that these reasons fall into three groups, which were explored in more depth in Chapter 7. Firstly, my reasons for being ethical might be based in society, and so I accept what it says (via laws and social norms) about things like killing and stealing.

Alternatively my reasons might be based on my regard for good relationships with other people, along with my experience that relationships tend to be better when my own actions are ethical. So, as part of this perspective on ethics, I would see that actions like killing and stealing are wrong.

The third reason for rejecting actions like killing and stealing is my perception of myself, my identity. At this level, those actions are wrong because they are against my idea of the kind of person I want to be. Again, this can go back to belief in a deity or to other grounds.

The lesson is that we cannot prove, to the satisfaction of all of these diverse people, that certain things are right or wrong. We can arrive at a conclusion personally, or for our social group, finding a position that is compelling to us, but beyond our self or our group, we can only offer reasons to others that we consider to be persuasive.

Within a given society there will be agreement about basic things, like killing and stealing, and these agreements are expressed in laws and the enforcement of those laws. Where there are disagreements between societies, say, if one society has a system of slavery and another society says this is wrong, we are left with the avenues just described. The legal argument does not hold, because laws are established within societies, not between them. The appeal to a deity probably does not hold, because the various societies may appeal to different holy texts, or different interpretations of those texts, or different understandings of who "God" is.

The only common ground between societies is that we are all human, and we all depend on planet earth to remain alive. This is not to say that the natural world compels us to hold certain values. Rather, it is to say that one of the unique aspects of humans, and one that all humans share, is the formulating of values to apply to themselves. So that when we want to argue that something is just right (or wrong), the common basis that we have across societies is our humanity. So it makes sense if the values we create are based on our desire, as humans, to survive, individually and collectively, and to enjoy life.

This is a conversation that needs to be built up between persons and societies; there can be no godly pronouncements. We have to establish what is our common ground, and what are our shared understandings of the world. Even to establish that we share a commitment to concepts of right and wrong at all is a work of conversation.

And if a particular society has, in our view, abominable practices and objectives, then it is a matter for our own society to determine, on the basis of its own accepted values, what it will do. This has been the rationale behind United Nations military interventions on many occasions – an agreement between UN members to enter a country by force in order to prevent human atrocities occurring.

This discussion also reminds us that when we talk about ethics and values, there are always two aspects, a negative and a positive. We can talk about certain types of actions as being wrong, but then we see that there is an aspirational aspect as well. As Jesus said to his listeners, you have the law that says you should not kill, but I say to you, love your enemies, and bless them that curse you.

When we accept the objective of living ethically, we certainly see that there are actions that we should not do, but we also come to see that at the heart of all those rules there is a positive admonition. It is not just that we should not kill, it is that we should positively foster the well-being of others, unselfishly. This goes beyond the province of the law, to a deeper appreciation of ethics.

Q 2. How does this framework of values help me to resolve my attitude towards things like money and power?

The framework does not, in itself, spell out rigid "answers" to questions like this. It is not intended to. In fact, what it highlights is that you have to work out for yourself what is appropriate for you in your context. The framework certainly doesn't say that money and power are "bad". But nor does it suggest that money and power are unconditionally "good".

How do the concepts help to clarify your attitude towards money, power, ambition and success? In Chapter 5 we saw that we all have aims in life. We are alive, and it is our nature to strive for six aims in life. Our individual emphasis will be different among those six aims, because of our needs, preferences and circumstances, but we all adopt some version of these various aims.

Money and power may be expressions of a particular aim. For example, money can be an expression of our mastery and independence, or it can be a signifier of our belonging and acceptance in society.

If we are to look at things like money, power, ambition and success in the light of ethics, then Chapter 3 is relevant. Ethics was defined there as having regard for the well-being of others and the natural world as well as our own well-being. What this perspective asks us to do is to see our desire for money, power and success in the light of the whole.

The extremes are, on the one hand, to take a survivalist viewpoint where we will destroy anything and anyone to get the most that we can, and on the other hand, to adopt the viewpoint of global harmony, where our actions are selfless and seek to serve the well-being of all. The shift from one end of the spectrum to the other involves an accumulation of faith, an inner knowing that our real needs will be provided for when we love all and serve all.

This is a dynamic picture. There is not one "right" answer. Each one of us has to work out for ourselves what is appropriate for us, and that will also change over time. There are social norms that, for example, disapprove of people who are very ruthless in business, and we can choose to be guided by those social norms. At the same time, we need to recognise that social norms are often only loose guides: the ruthless business person may be criticised, but such people are also tolerated, and even venerated if they are very successful. To be guided solely by social norms is to stand on rather shaky ground.

The approach presented in this book is evolutionary and developmental – it asserts that our quest is to expand our awareness and understanding, to question ourselves continually. The quest is to become more conscious of the whole (or all-that-is) and to bring our lives more into harmony with that. This moves us beyond social norms.

Society provides us with a bedrock of minimum standards for behaviour – our laws. Beyond that there are the social norms. And beyond that, there are our own choices about how we want to live our lives, about who we want to be. Ethics as the concern for adherence to moral rules evolves into the aspiration to penetrate into the essence of truth, peace, right action, love and insight.

Q 3. How do I make decisions on ethical issues?

This is a large issue which requires a long conversation. I devoted two out of ten chapters in *Human Values and Ethics in the Workplace* to ethical decision-making. The first observation to make is that decisions are made in various ways. There are:

- scripted, or routine, decisions,
- decisions in the context of relationships, and
- deliberated "policy" decisions.

The point of these distinctions is that there are some issues that strike us as significant and novel, and they need deliberate discussion and weighing of options so that we can formulate our "policy", while there are some issues that arise regularly and about which we have established rules (or scripts). All the while, we act in the midst of a web of relationships, and our actions have meaning in those contexts and serve to either strengthen or damage those relationships.

Accordingly, one aspect of making decisions ethically is the examination of our ordinary, scripted actions, to consider whether they reflect the values that we would want. Scripted actions are generally taken for granted and can embody attitudes that we are unaware of.

On the other hand, being conscious of our values and clear about our commitment to them can eliminate a great deal of angst in ethical decision-making. If you are clear that a certain action is wrong, then you will not be tempted to do it, even where the personal cost or the rewards seem high. If we always seek to act consistently with our values, much of the stress associated with making ethical decisions disappears.

The second aspect, relationships, is highlighted because our decisions and actions often have two effects. As well as achieving a goal, our actions affect relationships. It can be quite an art to ensure that a goal is attained and that a relationship is maintained as well. We often compromise one for fear of damaging the other, or damage one in order to achieve the other.

The third aspect, making decisions where time needs to be spent on considering all the factors and possible outcomes, is what people often mean when they talk about ethical decision-making. This is clearly necessary, but it is likewise important to recognise the other two aspects, as it is easy to overlook the fact that we are making decisions in those circumstances too.

We can make some basic statements about ethical decision-making, to put the process in context:

1. All situations are subject to ethical scrutiny, even routine ones where the content does not seem to be of great import.
2. Ethics must be an integrated part of all decision-making, not just for some situations that we deem to be ethically problematic.
3. An ethical decision-making model consists of both a process and a set of criteria for decisions, and the criteria are based on the human values.
4. Much decision-making is intuitive and expert-like rather than objective, detached and step-based, and it may involve imagination and innovation, not just adherence to moral rules.
5. Ethical dilemmas are about conflicts between ethical values, not about ethical choices that are difficult because high personal risks are involved.
6. Ethics is essentially a practical matter. The reason that decisions are important is because we intend to implement them, and they make a difference to our own life and other people's lives.
7. Perceptions are not "objective" truth. Our definition of the situation carries an implicit ethical stance. And how we perceive the problem is based on our current understanding and values.

It is worth emphasising the fifth statement. People often say they have an ethical dilemma, implying that the situation is ethically unclear, when what is really happening is that the ethics are very clear but the consequences are dire. If you discover that your manager is embezzling funds from the organisation, that is not an ethical dilemma. You know that it is wrong. What may be difficult is knowing how to go about addressing the situation without getting harmed yourself.

An ethical dilemma is when it is not so easy to see what is right, such as when two values seem to conflict with each other. For example, you are responsible for a person's performance (e.g. as a manager or a parent) and they are doing something wrong or poorly. But it is also important not to discourage them. How do you balance accountability for conduct, and encouragement of improvement? This is where ethics calls us to exercise wisdom.

The seventh statement also deserves emphasis. The way we perceive situations, and then describe them, is not neutral. People see and describe situations from the basis of their view of the world. When we come to evaluate the ethics of a situation, we need to be aware that our perception of it is imperfect.

We may miss seeing important factors, and we may not have taken different persons' perspectives into account. To put it more strongly, in the framework of personal growth, the situation may be presenting us with a challenge to our current attitudes. The constructive way to approach issues that strike us as being ethically potent is to humbly seek to improve our appreciation of all-that-is in the situation. This requires empathy and imagination. Then our actions might be quite different, and so may we.

Q 4. What do you do when two values conflict with each other?

The first thing that has to be said, and this applies to all thinking about ethical issues, is, always seek to think for yourself. Societies are generally strong on conventions, particularly conventions about morality, so it is always easier to conform to a conventional view about an ethical situation rather than pausing to think about what is really involved, and deciding for ourselves.

The second thing is, try to "think from the whole". There is a higher level at which everything moves in harmony. Seek to include all perspectives and accommodate all people. But, keep in mind that we do not find this place by compromising our principles. Sometimes we need to stand firm on a matter of principle, even if we have to stand alone.

When we are faced with what seems like a conflict of values, and it seems that there is no "right thing" to do, keep in mind that things will balance out in the bigger picture, *if* that is our intention. Create a whole in which everything has its place. That thought, held constantly, will become the reality.

The correct response, when faced with what seems irreconcilable, is to delve more deeply into the nature of the problem. This will make our choices clearer, and more in tune with the harmony of the whole. This exploration also requires us to be realistic about the situation and about ourselves.

Measure out what is possible; set limits. In resolving a conflict in values, do not be too harsh with yourself or others either. When in doubt about what to do, it is good to recall what the Dalai Lama says, that the core of his philosophy is kindness. Choose the course of action that furthers kindness.

The endeavour to determine what to do when we are faced with a conflict of values is necessary, and good, for our development. This work makes our understanding deeper and richer. Accordingly, we should pursue good actively. Part of ethics is about maintaining personal standards of behaviour, but the greater part of ethics is about making energetic progress in fostering good.

"Articulate what is right" is another aspect of addressing conflicts in values. Articulating a problem helps us to be clearer about what is at stake. Until we can say what is going on, clearly, we cannot make progress on resolving a situation. Not only that, but the very act of putting things into words starts us along the road to finding a resolution. It gets our thoughts going, and things begin to take shape.

Sometimes, it is true, it seems we are not allowed to be completely radiant. The circumstances militate against it. Our actions are not ideal, and the outcome is not ideal, in our eyes. Well, we are a work in progress. The injunction is, to go back to the reasons, delve more deeply into the causes, pare away what is unsatisfactory in ourselves, think from the whole, and trust that there is harmony in all-that-is.

Q 5. Given that there are different world views, who is to say what is ethical and what is not? Or what is virtuous and what is not? Is all ethics relative?

As we have said, we can assert that something is ethical or unethical. In social contexts, this assertion may meet with definite agreement, definite disagreement or something in between, a measure of doubt and uncertainty. The issue is to know what the grounds are for our assertions on ethics. What are the reasons for our assertion, beyond the fact that we feel strongly about the matter?

Even when people agree about the ethics of a particular act, their reasons may differ widely. Most people would agree that the gunman who walks into a café and randomly kills several people has committed a monstrously immoral act, a violation of our shared ethics. But delve for the reasons for the assertion and we find that people's reasons vary. And the various reasons can be plotted against the seven world views. Some will appeal to society's laws about the illegality of killing fellow citizens, others will appeal to the need for people to be able to trust fellow citizens not to harm them, others will say that killing a person is a violation of the oneness of all things. Some will express their reasons in terms of God's commandment not to kill, or in terms of a particular moral theory.

In many other cases, people's positions differ. If we look at the last thirty years in western societies, debate has raged and the weight of public opinion has shifted in areas such as whether it is morally acceptable for women to participate in the workforce, or for people to have single-sex relationships. And opinion is still volatile on these subjects. When we look to the reasons that people put forward to support their position, the reasons differ across the same spectrum as they do when talking about a random killer.

This is not to say that ethics is relative, if that means that my view of what is ethical is valid for me, and your view of what is ethical may be different but it is valid for you, and we cannot go any further than that. The framework presented in this book rejects that stance. We say that social groups, collectively, reach agreement about what is ethical, and establish laws to uphold the minimum level of behaviour indicated by that agreed view. It is a general platform, aimed at ensuring basic social functioning, not a refined guide for individual living, and as such it can be crude, and it embodies blind spots and injustices.

Despite the imperfections of the law (and many would say that their society's laws embody many injustices) the existence of the law is testimony to the fact is that societies have a level of social agreement about ethics. On this basis we could say that ethics is relative, because the views of a society, and its laws, change over time.

But it would be misleading to say that ethics is relative if that suggests that ethics is purely arbitrary, a creature of whim and idiosyncrasy. It is more accurate to see ethics as an evolutionary social process, where ethics is debated, experiences occur and are reflected upon, and understandings evolve. There is movement forwards and backwards, as people react to events with fear, courage or new insight.

Occasionally there are great insights that shift people forwards irrevocably, for example, the inclusion of women as voters. Whereas in the nineteenth century the accepted view was that it was not appropriate that women should vote, now it would seem preposterous if they did not. (This is not to say that societies generally have resolved all the issues related to the role of women in society.)

At the individual level a similar process occurs. Our ethics are "relative" in the sense that we work out our own values, subject to our upbringing, social influences, our circumstances and experiences, and our reflective thinking about all of this. Our ethics are not relative if that means that it doesn't matter what we believe or do. The truth is that we are located in this life at a certain point, and we can choose to live well, to live a life that grants us dignity in our own eyes, or we can live a lesser life. It is our choice whether or not to care.

The path of ethical development begins with opening our awareness to ourselves and our surroundings, to other people and the natural world. It proceeds via the recognition that other people are in essence facing the same life experience as we are; they are located as human beings in the same world, when external circumstance is stripped away.

The practice of this awareness carries us through the various levels of consciousness. As was described in the body of the book, step by step we see beyond our own physical needs to the security of our family, then to the nurture of further social groups, such as school, employer, and social organisations. As we become more aware of our own individuality, we distinguish ourselves from all of those groups and begin to stand on our own principles, our own unique vision of what life should be like.

Many people remain at a particular stage of consciousness and consolidate their understanding of that perspective. We can be content to be a loyal member of an organisation, a solid, law-abiding citizen, or a competent worker, manager or professional. But the vista of a larger, more inclusive view of the universe lies before us. And in that vista, we understand ethics as both a restraint on our behaviour (having regard for the well-being of others) and an aspiration to be all that we can be. This is the quest to delve into the deep meaning of the human values of truth, peace, right action, love and insight in our lives.

Q 6. How do I do my job in an organisation that has a different understanding of ethics than I do?

When we are in any situation where our understanding of what is ethically required is different from those around us, whether as an employee of an organisation, or in any other life situation, there are three types of responses that people commonly make: fight, flight or freeze. The issue may be how to keep our integrity, or how to prevent the organisation from causing harm to others, but our immediate response will be a quick consideration of these three options.

When we take time to reflect, the range of options is usually wider than this, and the choice becomes more subtle and complex. But it is still worth considering the three reactive choices. Moreover, we all have a history, and we can all undoubtedly find instances where we have taken one of these three options, and now we might think about it differently.

We may be ashamed of having run away from an ethical issue. We may be proud of having stood up and fought for what was right. And we may have frozen when faced with a big issue, and just pushed it to the side and carried on as if nothing was happening. And we may still not know what we should have done, because we may still feel that we were powerless to do anything effective.

None of these options is invariably the "right thing to do". Suppose we get a job with an organisation, and it turns out that the atmosphere is poisonous. Managers act rudely towards employees, they are harsh, unrealistic about tasks, and capricious in their decisions. Employees do not cooperate with each other or help each other.

What can you do about this? You might raise it at meetings and ask for better teamwork, caring and communication. You might discuss it with colleagues or your manager. Let's say you do this. As a result you are criticised and ostracised, including by your colleagues. Perhaps things will go better if you just accept the culture, and work quietly within it. Perhaps your modelling as a peaceful, considerate person will contribute to a slow change for the better in the atmosphere. Or perhaps you should leave. Simply look for another job, get out of there.

Where do ethics come into this? No one can give you a definitive answer that this or that course of action is the right thing to do. Only you can decide. Only you can weigh up the situation and make a judgement as to what is the best thing to do, having regard for your own well-being and that of others. Sometimes leaving is the best way to retain your integrity, sometimes you may think of another way to address the issue constructively.

One of the points to be made about these dilemmas is that being ethical is not just a sentimental preference for ethical behaviour. To live ethically requires us to build up skills in fostering ethical behaviour in organisations and other social contexts. We may need to:

- learn how to state a position clearly and confidently
- think through conversations and rehearse our responses to situations where we are pressured into doing something that is against our ethics
- be more innovative in how we guide groups towards better ethical norms
- work on the strengths require to maintain high ethical standards as a model for others.

When we confront obstacles and challenges, we may feel afflicted by them. This is a time to pause and re-imagine the situation. Rise above the situation and observe it as if from a tower. See the different participants and their points of view. Look for the possibility of a positive outcome. Look for common goals and principles and explore how you can work back from there to find a more congenial solution to the situation.

You may find that a particular value comes to the fore. Perhaps you have had an experience where you failed to have the courage to stand up for what was right. And now another situation arises where you are called to stand up for what is right. You know it is your courage that is being tested. So you act.

And maybe later you think that you could have dealt with the situation in a different way. But you did prove to yourself that you are able to act courageously, and this is what was the most important thing – this time, at least.

Search for people who can assist you in any way, people who may have a solution to the problem, and people who can sustain you in your commitment to acting ethically. Avoid the temptation to be the lonely, tragic hero. Above all, stay connected to the desire for the well-being of all. We are always connected to the creative spirit. All that happens eventually forms part of the Great Harmony. Stay tuned to that thought and you connect with what is truly great, and you will gather energy for decisive new moves.

Q 7. Is there a fundamental human value? Albert Schweitzer, for example, said that "reverence for life" is the fundamental human value.

We have presented a framework of values consisting of five core human values – truth, peace, right action, love and insight. But there is that story in the Bible where people asked Jesus what the greatest commandment was. To which Jesus responded by saying, "Love the Lord thy God with thy whole heart and with thy whole soul and with thy whole mind" and "love thy neighbour as thyself".

We might note that Jesus actually declined to reduce all the commandments to one commandment; he chose to focus on two commandments. Essentially, the issue at stake here is not about finding an answer that is "the truth", it is about finding an answer that is helpful. What Jesus said was helpful because it summed up a multitudinous set of rules with an essential principle, which was love. And he applied that principle to two domains: the divine essence of all-that-is, and our relationships with other people on this planet.

If we take each of the five core human values and sink deeply into them, we find that there is ultimately no difference between them – truth is peace is right action is love and insight. We explore them separately because our nature as humans is that we have a cognitive dimension, an emotional dimension, a moral valuing dimension, an energy/spirit dimension and a psyche (identity). Within this we are but one person.

Would we describe the fundamental human value differently to Schweitzer? Let's take our definition of ethics again: having regard for the well-being of others. It is this same concept that Schweitzer is expressing. He expresses it as strongly as possible, by saying we should have reverence for all life. It is not that the general intent of the two formulations is different. It is that Schweitzer's formulation is an exalted form of the intent, one that we would associate with the higher levels of consciousness.

The purpose of the five core human values approach to ethics is to resonate with the common ways that people characterise ethical situations and decisions. Ethics is not the province of philosophers who enjoy abstract moralising; it is the concern of all of us, it is about how each of us decides what to do in our everyday life. In exploring the human values approach we saw that there is an evolutionary pathway through various levels of consciousness. What ethics means to someone living out of a survivalist world view is different from what it is for a person who recognises the obligations of moral principles.

With this in mind, describing ethics as "having regard for the well-being of others" offers a language that carries meaning across all the levels. Whereas the language of reverence or love may be regarded as setting an unnecessarily high standard for the ordinary person who would be content to know how to be a good citizen in society, having regard for the well-being of others speaks to our common humanity. It implies that we all stand in the same place: we all have an equal right to exist, and it says there is an obligation on everyone, even those who don't care, to have regard for others.

Recall the quote from L.E. Modesitt: "All life is a struggle with ethics. Those who fail to understand that are doomed to destruction."

The path of ethical development begins with opening our awareness to ourselves and our surroundings, to other people and the natural world. It proceeds via the recognition that other people are in essence facing the same life experience as we are; they are located in the same way, when external circumstance is stripped away.

You could argue that ethics is not all of life. As a living being we desire to do many things, to be many things, and achieve many things, and ethics is the restraint on our behaviour. But if our desires are like the archer bending the bow, then it is ethics that directs the arrow to the right target. And so we say, there are two things in life, joy and correctness.

Acknowledgments and references

Many people have helped me to develop my ideas about ethics and human values, through events, through conversations and through pointers they gave me to writers who might be of interest. I thank you all. I am grateful for what I have received from you.

A great deal of reading preceded and contributed to the writing of this book. However, the intent was to present the ideas simply rather than burden their expression with a host of references. My book *Human Values and Ethics in the Workplace* offers a more extensive account of the ideas and includes references to source materials.

Glenn Martin, *Human Values and Ethics in the Workplace*, G.P. Martin Publishing, 2010. Available from www.lulu.com, www.amazon.com, or www.glennmartin.com.au.

References

The following books provided the quotations used in *The Little Book of Ethics*.

Dalai Lama, 1999, *Ancient Wisdom, Modern World: Ethics for the New Millennium*, Abacus, London.

Wayne Dyer, 2007, *Change Your Thoughts - Change Your Life: Living the Wisdom of the Tao*, Hay House, Carlsbad CA.

Pierro Ferrucci, 1983, *What We May Be*, Tarcher, New York.

Alfred Huang, 1998, *The Complete I Ching*, Inner Traditions International, Rochester VT.

Laotse, 1948, *The Wisdom of Laotse*, trans. Lin Yutang, The Modern Library.

L.E. Modesitt Jr, 2004, *The Ethos Effect*, Orbit, London.

Inazo Nitobe, 2011, *The Way of the Samurai*, Arcturus, London.

Your whole life

The beginning: awareness,
seeing the world as all-that-is,
then, as
I and not-I
seeing all-that-is as
what is and what is becoming
(what may be)
then, seeing
what is desirable and what is not,
and wanting my own good, my own satisfaction
and seeing how I exist among others
who are located in the same way as I,
amidst all-that-is.

Resolving to know,
to live knowingly,
to delve into all the depths and dimensions
of all-that-is
and be satisfied
with the desire to be one with all
and so to know, to feel,
to act, to enjoy
in all the realms and circumstances
of each day,
to ask what is helpful,
what is steadfast and upright,
and see what is enough
and know that it is sublime and abundant.

About the author

GLENN MARTIN (1950–) was born in Sydney, Australia and grew up there. He moved to the far north coast of New South Wales in the mid-1970s, seeking out a back-to-the-earth life style. He stayed in the area for 20 years, holding a variety of jobs: school teacher, community worker, social researcher and manager of organisations in the community sector.

His first two books were local histories: *Places in the Bush: A history of the Kyogle Shire* (1988) and *The Kyogle Public School Centenary Book* (1995).

After gaining a Bachelor of Business with First Class Honours and the University Medal from Southern Cross University, he returned to live in Sydney. He works as a writer, editor and consultant on human resources, employment law, training and development, and business ethics.

He has been the editor and principal writer for the CCH Australia publication, *Managing Training & Development* for over ten years. He has contributed chapters on human resources, training and ethics to several CCH Australia books, including the *Australian Master Human Resources Guide*. He was the editor for *Training & Development in Australia* for five years. He currently edits the journal and other publications for Spirituality, Leadership and Management Inc.

He wrote and published a book on ethics in 2007: *Human Values and Ethics in the Workplace* (updated in 2010). He has released two collections of poems and personal stories: *Flames in the Open* and *Love and Armour*.

Glenn's first novel was *The Ten Thousand Things: A story of the lived experience of the I Ching* (2010). His second novel is *Sustenance* (2011).

His websites are www.ethicsandvalues.com.au and www.glennmartin.com.au.

ORDER FORM

Order by email: info@glennmartin.com.au

Order from website: www.glennmartin.com.au

Order by post: G.P. Martin Publishing

5 Gumnut Place, Cherrybrook NSW 2126 AUSTRALIA

Order by fax: 61 (0)2 9945 0524

Please send me prices + postage on the following books:

Book	Quantity
The Little Book of Ethics: A human values approach	
The Ten Thousand Things: A story of the lived experience of the I Ching	
Human Values and Ethics in the Workplace	
Sustenance	
Flames in the Open	
Love and Armour	

Discounts available for bookshops and wholesale purchasers.

Name: ....

Address: ....

....

Town/city: ....

Country: .... ZIP/Postcode: ....

Phone: .... Mobile: ....

email: ....

www.ingramcontent.com/pod-product-compliance
Lightning Source LLC
Chambersburg PA
CBHW032019090426
42741CB00006B/661